the COURSE of your LIFE

A personal revolution

Leader's Guide

Tony Payne

The Course of Your Life: Leader's Guide
© Matthias Media 2011

Matthias Media
(St Matthias Press Ltd ACN 067 558 365)
PO Box 225
Kingsford NSW 2032
Australia
Telephone: (02) 9663 1478; international: +61-2-9663-1478
Facsimile: (02) 9663 3265; international: +61-2-9663-3265
Email: info@matthiasmedia.com.au
Internet: www.matthiasmedia.com.au

Matthias Media (USA)
Telephone: 330 953 1702; international: +1-330-953-1702
Facsimile: 330 953 1712; international: +1-330-953-1712
Email: sales@matthiasmedia.com
Internet: www.matthiasmedia.com

ISBN 978 1 921896 33 0

Cover design and typesetting by Matthias Media.

Contents

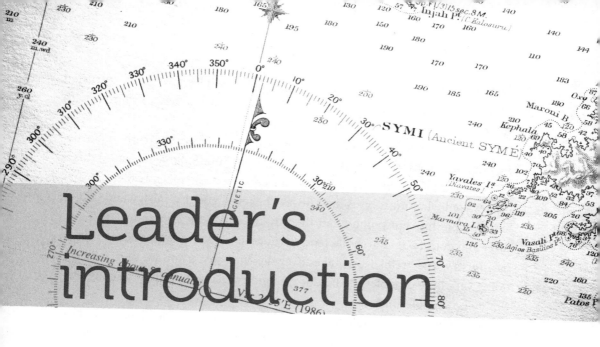

Leader's introduction

1. How to get started

- If you want to, you can watch the two introductory video clips on the DVD—entitled 'What is *The Course of Your Life?*' and 'How **not** to use this course'.
- Read the introduction below. Some of the material (especially in points 2 and 3) is covered more briefly in the two introductory clips.
- Do some planning about how you are going to use the course in the context of your ministry.

2. The pressing need

A couple of years ago, I accidentally wrote a bestseller. Colin Marshall and I put out a small and uncomplicated book called *The Trellis and the Vine*,[1] in which we argued from Scripture that all Christians are involved in God's great work in the world. We are all not only disciples but also makers and growers of other disciples—each in our own way, according to our circumstances, opportunities and gifts.

This is hardly an earth-shattering idea, nor are we the first ones to highlight it. From our Reformation heritage, evangelicals have long believed that there are not two kinds of Christian—the priests and the rest of us. We believe

---

1 Matthias Media, Sydney, 2009.

there is only one kind of disciple, and that all disciples have been entrusted with the word of God, not only to read and obey it but also to share it with others for their conversion and edification.

However, to believe this is true is one thing. To allow that truth to permeate our churches and our lives is something else. And (in large measure) this is why *The Trellis and the Vine* struck such a chord with so many readers. It simply restated what most of us have always believed about ministry and church and discipleship, but pointed out the ways in which the programs and structures and culture of church life tend to squeeze out this people-focused vision of ministry. The 'trellis work' takes over the 'vine work', and we find ourselves doing very little disciple-making, nor training and equipping of the congregation to be disciple-makers.

As Colin and I have talked about this with pastors and leaders around the world, one very common issue emerges. Many are keen to begin the difficult process of refocusing their congregational life on people and 'vine work' rather than on structures and programs. But the first pressing question is: **How can we convey this vision to the congregation? We may be keen to train people as disciple-making disciples, but what if they are not so keen?** What if they already feel busy and over-overcommitted? How can we fire up people with the desire and commitment to give themselves to God's work in the world: to making and growing disciples of Jesus? How can we inspire them with the vision of how great God's plans are, and how extraordinary it is that we have a part to play in them—that we **all** have a part to play? **How can we get our people to take their eyes off their small ambitions and their daily struggles, and catch the vision of being a disciple-making disciple in every aspect of their lives?**

This is not a structural problem, nor one that can be solved by better programs or snazzier church services or more impassioned appeals by the pastor for people to "get involved". It's a **heart** problem. It's about what our people passionately believe to be important. And therefore it is also a mind problem—since what we really love and long for (our heart's desire) is inextricably connected with how we view the world and ourselves, and what we think is important. It's connected with our (usually unexamined) mental models of the world.

If we want to see our congregational life change, and individual members give themselves to being disciple-making disciples, we need to see hearts change. **We need to blow people's minds with the wonder of God and the gospel, and to fire their hearts with a new love and joy and enthusiasm for serving Christ not only as a disciple but also as a disciple who longs to make and grow other disciples.**

How do we do this? How does that kind of revolution happen? Well, only two things are needed: the word of God and the Spirit of God. The Bible tells us that the word of God is the sword by which the Spirit of God transforms minds, changes hearts, and produces the fruit of a changed life. If we want to see people change, we need to dig deeply into the Scriptures.

We also need to be deep in prayer, because only the work of God's own Spirit will skewer our hearts with the word of God and bring real change. We need to beg God by his Spirit to work in the hearts of people.

We also need to recognize that proclaiming the word of God to people almost always involves both a negative and positive aspect. The Spirit uses the Word as a sword to hack away at the false and misleading ideas we have in our minds, and to refashion our thinking in line with God's reality. Like Paul in 2 Corinthians 11, then, there is some dismantling and demolishing that needs to be done in people's thinking, along with rebuilding. We need to get behind the defences that people often set up (even without realizing it).

Lastly, we need to work closely and individually with people. Real progress in people's lives almost always happens in close relationship, not in a big crowd.

This comes back to our impatience for change and growth. We want to transform everyone, and quickly! We want an immediate answer, a new program, a quick solution. But that's not how people change and grow. It happens over time as the Word penetrates people's minds, along with much prayer and personal connection.

3. So why this course?

You will note that I have not suggested that the particular resource you have in your hands is necessary for this task—because it isn't. All you really need for the task of making disciples (and disciple-makers) is the word of God and prayer ministered in relationship over time.

However, if we can help each other do this by sharing wisdom, then that is also a gift from God. And that's why I've written *The Course of Your Life*—as a framework to help you apply the word of God to people's lives prayerfully and intensively to see them grow as disciple-making disciples.

In particular, the primary aim of this course is to revolutionize people's understanding of who God is, what he has done in Christ, what his extraordinary plans are for the world, and how that relates to each of our lives. I want to set people's minds on fire with the wonder of who Christ is, and what a radical and extraordinary thing it is to live as his disciple.

In other words, the course aims to do what is often difficult to do in week-by-week sermons or in regular small group Bible studies. It aims to focus intently and intensively on the central and profound issues of Christian life and discipleship, and to revolutionize people's minds and hearts by bringing the Bible's teaching together in a focused and compelling way.

Another way of describing what this course is trying to do is to say that it is seeking by the work of God's Spirit to change head, heart and hands:

- Head: the course seeks to revolutionize people's minds with God's worldwide plans in Christ.
- Heart: the course seeks to do this in such a way as to motivate and inspire.
- Hands: the course seeks to impart a basic ministry skill (of how to read the Bible one-to-one with someone else).

This course is simply a useful framework to help you raise up disciple-making disciples in your congregation through God's word and prayer.

4. The three basic strands of the course

Before looking at the mechanics of how you might run the course, it's worth understanding the three main components or strands of the material and how they fit together.

A. The seminars

The nine seminars are where the core content is delivered. They are designed to contain around 90 minutes of content, although you may want to add discretionary time at the beginning for drinks/snacks and chatting, plus some informal time for talking and packing up at the end.

Exactly when and how you run the seminars will obviously depend on the people doing the course, and how many there are of them. If your participants are workers, you may wish to run the seminars from 7-9 pm and start with some finger food (so that people can come straight from work if they wish). If you're running it with college or university students, you may want to put the seminars on at the end of the day (e.g. 4-6 pm) and conclude with dinner.

Each seminar includes various Bible research activities as well as some video-based input that summarizes and pulls together the ideas. Using these video segments has some obvious advantages—it makes the course easier to run, it maintains a consistent quality, and it allows the group to interact with the material a bit more freely (because they're disagreeing with the person on the screen, not the person standing right in front of them).

However, please feel free to teach some or all of these input segments yourself. The video scripts are provided in full in this leader's guide, so you can use them as a base for preparing your own talk. PowerPoint slides for the diagrams are also available on *The Course of Your Life* website.[2]

Some of the Bible study and discussion activities are best done in smaller subgroups (and you will see suggestions on the way through where this is the case), but these groups do not have to be the same each week. If you have less than six people doing the course, you will do better to stay in one group for most of the activities.

B. The intensive

The course includes an intensive between seminars 8 and 9. In most contexts, this will work best as two full days away together. A Friday and Saturday works very well—that is, arriving on Thursday evening or first thing Friday morning, and then going home after an early dinner on Saturday. This allows people to be back for church on Sunday and not to be away from their families for the whole weekend.

It is also possible to run the intensive as two separate days (e.g. on consecutive Saturdays), or to run it without going away somewhere—that is, to work through the material on consecutive days, with participants going home to sleep. But if you can manage to stay at least one night together in a venue away from home, it really is of enormous benefit. It builds relationships, and allows more time and 'space' to think and talk.

However you decide to run it, make sure that those who are going to participate in the course are committed to the dates you have set down for the intensive **before they agree** to do the course. The intensive is a vital component. It brings all the material together and allows people the time to think it through, to integrate the ideas, to talk about the implications and to pray together.

C. The one-to-one meetings

For the duration of the course, participants meet together regularly for an hour or so in pairs for Bible reading and prayer. So once you have finalized the group numbers, sort people into same-gender pairs for these one-to-one meetings (and as the leader, you should be in one of the pairs, or more than one if that is necessary). Do your best to pair people up according to where they live or work, to make it easier for them to find a convenient time.

----

2 www.matthiasmedia.com/courseofyourlife

The one-to-one meetings serve three important functions:

- **They provide a different level for getting into God's word.** The seminars work through lots of different Bible passages, pulling together some of the major themes and topics of the Bible. But in the one-to-one meetings, participants work through just one book of the Bible (Colossians), which provides the opportunity to delve more deeply into individual passages. Many of the ideas that come up in Colossians supplement and support the material in the seminars.
- **They offer an opportunity for mutual encouragement and challenge.** As participants get to know each other in the one-to-one pairs, they can talk and pray together about what they are learning in the course.
- **They teach a basic ministry skill.** By the end of this course, the participants will have learned how to read the Bible one-to-one with someone else. The ten one-to-one readings are really a mini training course in different ways to read the Bible one-to-one. Without realizing it, participants will have gained the skills, knowledge, experience and confidence in how to get together with another person and build them up in Christ through one-to-one Bible reading and prayer.

5. How to run the course

A. How **not** to use this course

Before looking at the various ways you might use this material, it's important to say something about how **not** to use it. If you are the pastor of a church, the temptation with any course like this is for it to become the latest in a long line of programs that you run for a while, trying to generate some enthusiasm for it before moving on to the next one when this one runs out of steam.

Try to resist the temptation simply to push as many people as possible through *The Course of Your Life* as quickly as possible in the hope of transforming your church in 12 months. Not only will this sort of approach almost certainly not work, it will become rapidly counter-productive. Your people will become increasingly jaded as each year rolls around and a new 'silver bullet' course or program is rolled out, with the promise that this is the one that will really make a difference.

That is not how ministry works. It's not how people change and grow. Real, substantial, lasting growth happens as the Word is applied prayerfully in personal relationship over time. A course like this one (and this is true of any framework or resource or set of ideas you might use) is not a substitute for the steady, consistent people-focused work of training people as disciples and disciple-makers. But it may be a very useful tool for doing that training.

B. How to use this course

The best way to use *The Course of Your Life* is broadly… but patiently. It is certainly not a course just for 'the elite'. Over time, it could become a basic framework that you want as many people as possible in your congregation to work through. Potentially, it is a course for everyone. But if you try to push everyone through it quickly, you will almost certainly fail because people need time—time to think and work the ideas through in their lives; time to change old habits and ways of thinking; time to gain confidence in their ability to minister to others.

Someone needs to stick with them as they do this; to keep reading and praying and talking; to keep mentoring and advising and following up. This is what training is like. It requires a trainer as well as a trainee. There are no shortcuts and no quick fixes.

However, the word and Spirit of God are immensely powerful. Over time, they can do what no program or structure or ministry fad can do—and that is profoundly change the hearts and minds and lives of God's people.

If you are the pastor or assistant pastor of a congregation, or a ministry leader of some kind (say, leading a Bible study group, or involved in a youth ministry or women's ministry or student/campus ministry), and you would like to see real change of the kind we are talking about, then you need to think in years—not weeks or months. Here's one approach:

> **Phase 1:** gather 8-10 reasonably solid, mature Christians and work
> through *The Course of Your Life* at a pace that is most appropriate (see
> options below). This may take ten weeks or four months—the time is
> not important. Once you've finished working through the course, spend
> some more time digging further into the Bible together and building on
> the basics—for example, starting to do some one-to-one Bible reading
> with others and encouraging each other in that; working through some
> other training material together (like *Two Ways to Live: Know and share
> the gospel*); or sending down deeper roots into Christian doctrine. (For
> further suggestions of how to build a one-year basic training program
> with resources from Matthias Media, see appendix 2.) You may spend a
> whole year doing all this. But the aim is train 8-10 people whose minds
> and hearts have been changed, and who want to grow other disciple-

making disciples of Jesus.[3]

Of course, if you are part of a church with other staff members or key lay leaders who would be capable of leading such a group, you could start with multiple groups of this size. (For example, there might be pre-existing small groups with good quality leaders who would be able to run the course, or who would welcome you joining them for 3-6 months to work through the course material.) If you had multiple groups running the course, you could all meet together as a group of 20-30 for the first 10-12 weeks to work through *The Course of Your Life* and then split into smaller groups to carry it further for the rest of the year.

Or you could kick the process off in the middle of your year, with the aim of spending six rather than 12 months together. There are numerous ways to do it.

At the end of this first phase, work out what comes next for those you have been working with. Are some of them ready to lead others through *The Course of Your Life*? Are some ready to start following up fringe people and newcomers? Or do one-to-one Bible studies with new or young Christians? Or lead a small Bible study group? Or…?

Phase 2: Choose the more mature and gifted people from your original group, and get them to start another two *Course of Your Life* groups (with you mentoring and supporting). You would also need to keep meeting (say every month, one-to-one) with the rest of your original group to support and coach them in the ministries they are pursuing.

Phase 3: You might now have 30 people who have been through *The Course of Your Life*, and have taken the time to consolidate the ideas and begin to put them into practice. This might have taken you two or three years, or even longer. Where you take it from here depends on the kinds of basic ministry structures you are working with. For example, as well as continuing to train others using *The Course of Your Life*, you could think of deploying your 30 well-trained people in one of two ways:

- as small group 'shepherds': to lead a group of 8-10 people and be responsible for their growth as disciple-making disciples (through meeting regularly as a small group, and through other personal contact)

---

3   This is what *The Trellis and the Vine* calls the "pastor's training team"—a group of people who begin to work alongside the pastor in 'vine work'.

- as 'sheepdogs': those who chase and follow up visitors, newcomers and non-Christian contacts (by meeting with them, reading the Bible with them, and seeking to move them towards Christ and maturity in him). One of the goals of the 'sheepdog' might be to connect people with one of the small groups and see them safely under the care of a small group 'shepherd'.

This is just one set of ideas to get you thinking, but I hope the principle is clear: don't use this course as a quick-fix program; **use it over time to begin to build a team of fellow workers in the gospel whose hearts have been fired with the vision of disciple-making**. Don't simply run people through the course and then move on to the next thing—you need to stick with the people. This will most often mean using the course as part of a longer-running group.

C. Different ways to run *The Course of Your Life*
The course consists of three strands of material (as we've just described):
- nine seminar-style sessions
- a two-day intensive
- nine one-to-one Bible readings.

Exactly how you weave these strands together, over what period of time and in what combination, is entirely up to you. You need to make a judgement about what will work best in your particular circumstances with your particular people. Here are three examples of how you could do it in three different time frames.

i. Over nine or ten weeks

- Each week, participants come to a seminar (around 90 minutes).
- Each week, participants also meet one-to-one with someone else in the group for around an hour (at a time and place of mutual convenience).
- Between seminars 8 and 9, you conduct the intensive as a two-day event (away for a weekend together, or Friday-Saturday).

This is the most time-intensive way to use the material, but is also usually the most effective. By doing the one-to-one meetings concurrently with the seminars, the content of the readings reinforces the seminar material. And by having the seminars follow one after the other each week, a real momentum is built as one concept builds on the next.

If you think your people can rise to this level of commitment, then I would strongly recommend using the material this way. It communicates that the subject matter of the course is something special and serious—something worth devoting extra time to over a nine-week period.

ii. Over 18 weeks or more

- Instead of running the seminars and one-to-one readings concurrently, you could interweave them. One week you do a seminar, and the following week participants do their one-to-one readings—either each pair could sort out their own time and place for the one-to-one meeting, or you could continue to meet altogether at your usual time and place (i.e. starting together as a group for some prayer and catch-up before splitting into pairs for the one-to-one component).
- The intensive could be run as a two-day event (as above), or on consecutive Saturdays (say from 9 am till 3 pm).

This is a less demanding way to run the material, and it allows you to fit all the content into a normal week-by-week timeslot. You won't gain quite the same synergy and momentum of doing it all concurrently, but then again there is more time to digest the material and let it soak in. This comes down to a judgement about what you think will work best with your participants.

iii. As a week-long conference or camp

- If you could take a group of people away for five days, then it would be possible to cover a great deal of the course material in one hit. You might not get through it all, but you could cover a lot of ground together.
- This would potentially be very powerful in helping people think through the big issues together, away from the distractions of daily life.
- However, it would be vital to make this sort of conference or camp the basis for an ongoing group or set of groups. Participants would receive a 'turbo boost' by going to a week-long conference, but you would need to stick with them over the following weeks and months to work it all out in practice.
- For the material to work in this way, the role of the regular seminars and the intensive would need to be reversed—that is, it would make sense to use the conference to cover all the main material in the seminars, with all its cumulative power and impact, and then to use weeks subsequent to the conference to complete the material in the intensive at a steady pace, thinking through and consolidating the implications. Here's an example of how you could run the course in this way:

	Day 1	Day 2	Day 3	Day 4	Day 5
Morning	Arrive and register	Seminar 2 Seminar 3	Seminar 5 Seminar 6	Seminar 7 Seminar 8	Intensive 2 121 meeting
Afternoon	Seminar 1 121 meeting	121 meeting	121 meeting	121 meeting	Depart
Evening	Free	Seminar 4	Q & A time	Intensive 1	

Then in subsequent weeks you would do:

- Intensive parts 3-6
- Seminar 9
- 121 readings alongside or interspersed.

Again, these are three suggestions that could work well for you depending on your circumstances. But feel free to take the strands and the framework and come up with your own creative way of utilizing the material.

6. Nuts and bolts

A. Who to invite

In a sense, this is a course for every Christian—because it is about the normal Christian life. It aims to demonstrate that the course of the normal Christian life is one where we not only strive towards maturity in Christ ourselves, but where we long to see others grow to maturity as well. In this sense, it's not really designed to be an evangelistic program for outsiders or for those on the fringes of our congregations who are still some distance from the kingdom. It's aimed at the large majority of people in our churches who are Christian but have not yet really grasped what it means to be a 'disciple-making disciple'.

This may leave you thinking, "Well, I can think of lots of those! Who should I invite to do the course?"

Again, this relates to your larger purpose in training a team of disciple-making disciples (as we've discussed above). The best people to start with are probably those whom you think have the most potential to join you in training others.

B. How to invite

Before you issue invitations for people to join a group in which you'll be running *The Course of Your Life,* make sure you've nailed down the key details—in particular, the venue and dates for the intensive. It is important that people know exactly what they're signing up for, and are willing to commit the necessary time. Make this really clear when you're talking to people about doing the course—they need to give a firm commitment, including to the intensive and the one-to-one meetings.

A useful way to handle the invitation process is to send a course brochure to people with a cover letter explaining why you're inviting them and what the key dates are, and mentioning that you will follow up with a call in the near future. A sample brochure and invitation letter are available for download at the website for the course.[4]

Instead of (or as well as) a brochure, you could also send people a link to the course invitation video. This is also available on the course website, as well as on the course DVD under 'Extra videos'.

C. What you'll need

You will need:

- a workbook for each person
- a leader's guide (the leader does not also need a workbook)
- a leader's DVD (assuming you want to use the video input clips).

You might also want to download other material (such as sample invitation brochures) from *The Course of Your Life* website: www.matthiasmedia.com/courseofyourlife

For each seminar, you will need access to a computer/projector or to a decent-sized TV if you are going to use the provided video segments.

The leader's guide contains all the material in the workbook, plus notes and scripts for the leader in **blue**.

7. The logic

Below is a summary of the main biblical ideas that the course seeks to cover, and the order and logic that connects them.

Seminar 1: Getting started

The course of our lives is determined by who we are (our background, nature, relationships, etc.) and where we are headed (our purpose, future, goals, dreams). Who are you? Where have you come from? Where are you headed?

This seminar aims to open up these ideas, and help participants start to get to know one another.

---

4   www.matthiasmedia.com/courseofyourlife

Seminar 2: God's creative purposes

To understand ourselves and our destiny we need to start with creation, for we are all creatures of the one good and sovereign God. God is the potter, we are the clay, and he made us intentionally and deliberately. His purposes for us are outlined in Genesis: to be fruitful and multiply, to fill the earth and subdue it, to have dominion over all other living things.

This means that the rationale for our lives—who we are, and why we are on this planet—is not self-generated. We don't impart meaning to our own lives. God our creator writes our mission statement and determines the course of our lives. And this grates against most of our deepest and most basic human beliefs.

Seminar 3: What went wrong?

We don't like bowing to God's rule. Adam and Eve didn't like it, and so they rebelled and were judged. They decided to write their own rules—to break God's rule—so they were judged and cast out. This is now who we are: rebels under judgement, excluded/alienated from God and his purposes, and under the reign of decay and death.

What does this mean for God's purposes? They seem to be frustrated. God's plan seems to have gone off the rails almost as soon as it got under way.

What does this mean for us and for our lives? The world we live in and the course of our lives is described perfectly in Ecclesiastes. We sense meaning but we can't properly grasp it, and it all seems absurd. We need to feel the weight of this: the frustration and unpredictability of human life; the universality of injustice, evil and death; the foolishness of thinking that we can sort out our own lives and control them.

Seminar 4: God's answer

There is an answer to the death, decay and absurdity of this fallen world and our lives. God's purposes are not frustrated. God's answer is revealed first in the Old Testament and then finally and majestically through his Son (Heb 1:1-4).

If God's answer to sin and evil and death is found in the Scriptural revelation culminating in Jesus, then this has radical implications for how we think about our lives. What God says is not an additional item to be fitted into the busy agenda of our lives. Instead, it completely rewrites the agenda of our lives. (This seminar is really about the sufficiency of Scripture.)

Seminar 5: God's agenda

So what is God's agenda for the world and for our lives? The Bible reveals that his big purpose is found in Christ—in fact, Christ **is** the purpose, the rationale, the agenda.

Passages such as Acts 17:22-31, Ephesians 1:1-10, Colossians 1:1-20 and Titus 2:11-14 reveal that God's agenda or purpose is history-long and world-wide. God has sent his Son Jesus into the world as a man to be the Christ and ruler of a new kingdom, to which redeemed and purified people from every nation (not just Israel) will belong. He has sent his Son to be the king of a new kingdom of God, a new creation, where there is no sin or pain or suffering or decay or death. Summary: God's agenda is to glorify Jesus the Christ by transferring forgiven rebels like us out of the domain of darkness and into his eternal kingdom.

Seminar 6: Christ's death, my life

How does God's agenda connect with the course of our lives? The answer lies in understanding the key moment in God's plan: the death and resurrection of Jesus.

Jesus died as our **substitute**, taking upon himself God's anger at our sin, and bringing us justification and redemption and reconciliation with God. But Jesus also died as our **representative**—that is, his death was our death (2 Cor 5:14-15; Gal 2:20). This means that when we are united with Christ by faith— that is, when we become Christians—a whole new life begins. Our old life is dead and gone, and we are raised up to lead a new life in which we live for the One who for our sake died and was raised.

So we actually have two lives: our old rebellious life that was crucified with Christ; and a completely new life that we now live by faith in the Son of God. It is the course of this new life that is now our concern.

Seminar 7: Transformation

Question: if our old life has been crucified with Christ, why do we still sin? Answer: it is because of the 'now' and 'not yet' nature of the kingdom of the Son. We have been transferred to his kingdom (past tense) and we are now raised up with Christ and seated with him (Eph 2:1-7)—but there is a delay, an overlap, in which we continue to live in a sinful world, and in a sinful body with a sinful mind, as we wait for the return of Jesus.

And so God's agenda for our lives is not just to transfer us to the kingdom of his Son, but also to transform us to be mature in Christ as we wait for his return. The new life we now live 'in Christ' is a life of killing off sin and clothing ourselves with the character of Christ. A fuller summary of God's agenda for the course of our new lives in Christ is: to **transfer** forgiven rebels like us out of the domain of darkness and into his eternal kingdom, and to **transform** us towards maturity in Christ as we wait for his return.

Seminar 8: God's method

Taking a step back: how does God achieve his agenda in the world? What is his method or strategy for transferring and transforming?

Essentially it comes down to three P's: **proclamation** of God's word, **prayer** for the Spirit to work, and **people** (who do the proclaiming and praying). It is the privilege and responsibility of every Christian to be part of God's agenda in the world—not only by seeking maturity in Christ in our own lives, but also by building others towards maturity in him.

How do we do this?

- We move ourselves towards maturity in Christ by prayerfully setting our minds on Christ and his word.
- We move others towards maturity in Christ by prayerfully speaking God's word to them.

Intensive

So far, we have seen that God has an agenda for the course of our lives (to transfer and to transform), and that we put that agenda into practice in our lives by striving towards maturity in Christ in our own lives, and by seeking to move others forward towards maturity in Christ as well.

But how does this overriding agenda in our lives intersect with our everyday life at home? At work? At church?

Seminar 9: Where to now?

Given all that we have learned, how do we start to implement this new vision for the course of our lives?

In particular, who are the people (in our work, family and church lives, both Christian and non-Christian) we are going to pray for, and seek to move towards maturity in Christ?

The one-to-one skills that participants have been learning will be invaluable in this.

8. A final word about prayer

Earlier in this introduction I noted that this course is by no means the only way to go about the task of training disciple-making disciples. I said "All you really need for the task of making disciples (and disciple-makers) is the word of God and prayer ministered in relationship over time".

The often-forgotten word in that sentence is 'prayer'. We all know the importance of prayer. We all recognize that our task is not only to speak God's word but also to pray that God would accompany his word with his life-giving, life-changing Spirit. And yet for most us, this recognition rarely translates into very much praying.

Let me encourage you: set aside time to pray for the people you're inviting to do the course. Pray for them before they begin the course, pray for them as they go through the course, and pray before every seminar that God would drive his word home into the hearts of those present, and profoundly change their lives.

You can also demonstrate the importance of prayer throughout the course by not short-changing time for prayer during the seminars (as we so easily do). Show people that the course of their life is shaped by making prayer a priority.

Seminar 1
Getting started

About this seminar

This first seminar is a little longer than the others, mainly because it has two important aims. It aims firstly to introduce the framework and goals of the course, to inspire and enthuse the participants about what is to come, and to communicate how it's all going to work—including some basic training in how to conduct the one-to-one meetings. This needs time.

But there is a second aim as well: to help your group begin to bond together. Even if the participants already know each other to some extent (e.g. from existing church relationships), it is important that they feel comfortable with each other and are willing and able to talk freely about their lives, their dreams and their struggles. This also needs time. This is why we recommend that you allow a little longer for this opening session—perhaps up to three hours.

Before the seminar, make sure you have worked out the one-to-one pairings. As the leader, you should be in one of the pairs (or more than one if that is necessary).

It would be an excellent idea to begin or conclude this opening session with a meal. Some ideas:

- Run it on a Saturday morning, starting with breakfast at 8 am and finishing with morning tea at around 10:30 am. (Or start with morning tea at 10:30 am and finish with lunch at around 1 pm.)
- Run it on a Sunday afternoon, starting with afternoon tea at 3:30 pm and concluding with dinner at around 6 pm.

- Run it on a Monday night, starting with a light meal at 6:30 pm and concluding with supper at around 9 pm.

You may wish to get more creative and run this opening seminar in conjunction with a more extensive social event that suits the group of people doing the course—a game of football, a craft morning, a trip to the movies, a round of golf, lunch out at a restaurant, and so on.

1. Introductions

The idea is to break the ice and begin to get comfortable with each other. If you are starting the session with a meal, this discussion could take place during the mealtime.

Timing: 45 minutes

A. A quick get-to-know-you quiz

Introduce yourselves by getting each person in the group to answer the following three questions in no more than 60 seconds:
- What's your full name (including middle name/s)?
- Where do you live now and with whom?
- Can you name a book, movie or TV show you have enjoyed in the last three months?

B. Thinking about your life

Now take it in turns to answer one of the following two questions (no more than three minutes for each person). Group members are allowed to ask follow-up questions.
- What have been the turning points in your life so far—the key moments when the road has taken a turn?
- Can you name one or two people (excluding your parents and God) who have had the most influence (for good or ill) in making you into the person you are today? How have they influenced you?

C. Pray

Two or three of the group who feel comfortable to do so can lead in prayer:
- giving thanks for this opportunity to pause and reconsider where our lives are headed
- praying for the members of the group by name, asking God to give insight and clarity and conviction over the duration of the course.

2. Input: Why are we here?

Play video clip 1 here, or give your own talk based on its content.

Timing: 7-10 minutes

Script:

Do you ever stop and think about where your life is going?

We don't do this most of the time. It would be unhealthy if we did. We can hardly conduct a full enquiry into the meaning of our existence every morning before we get out of bed.

But most people stop and think about their lives from time to time. We pause and take our bearings. Is my life where I thought it would be now? Is there some sort of overriding purpose? Where is it all going? Where am I going?

Sometimes grief or failure or a scare with illness pushes us to these thoughts.

Sometimes it just happens naturally at different times of life—like when we leave school, or when we turn 50.

Of course, there's a deeper and more pressing reason for stopping to ponder the course of our lives—it's the wonderful possibility that our lives do in fact have a profound purpose; that we were made by God for a reason. If that was the case, would you want to discover that purpose, that reason, and live the rest of your life pursuing it?

That's what this course is really about. It's an opportunity for you to pause and 'take the temperature' of your life: to think about who you are and why God put you here on this planet.

More specifically, *The Course of Your Life* is designed to help you achieve three things:

- To understand afresh who God is, what he is doing in our world, and what Jesus Christ has to do with that.
- To see and understand yourself afresh—who you really are, what you're here for, and what your future holds.
- On the basis of both of these things, to discover what God wants you to do with the rest of your life from this point on—not just in a vague general sense ('give him the glory', 'be a good Christian'), but more personally and specifically.

Your group leader will explain more about the nuts and bolts of how this will work in just a moment…

But in the meantime, you need to recognize at the outset that this is not a light or small thing you will be doing as a group over the next several sessions. These are hardly small or inconsequential topics. And there is every chance that as a result of what you do together during this time, your life will never be the same again—because you are going to be delving into what God has to say about the purpose and direction of your life.

But you should also recognize at the start that because the subject is so important and so personal, there will be times during the course when you will find it hard going. This may simply be because you find the content confusing or disturbing or unsettling. Some cherished ideas or assumptions might be challenged. Or you might long for a nice simple answer but find that none seems available. You won't find all the answers in the first week, or even by halfway through. Be patient, and keep searching and asking and grappling with the ideas.

But doing a course like this can be unsettling in another way. It can profoundly challenge not just our understanding but also our hearts and wills. It can call into question the very way we live our lives; our dreams, our goals, the things we love and long for. Be prepared for this, and pray that God would soften your heart to respond to his word.

3. Three gifts and three strands

Read through the following material with the group, pausing to clarify and answer questions as you go.

Timing: 20 minutes

A. Three gifts

You've just heard a summary of what this course is about. Another way of summarizing the methodology of this course is that we will be trying to make the most of three incredible gifts that God has given us:

- God has given us **his word**, the Bible, to light our path like a torch on a dark night. It is good to share our thoughts, feelings and experiences—but in the end it's God who not only has the answers, but also knows which are the truly important questions.
- God also gives us **each other**—to help, to urge, to encourage and to sharpen each other. You'll spend lots of time in the Bible during this course, and you'll do most of it together rather than individually.
- We also need God to work in our hearts and minds to help us understand and change. That's why **prayer** is such a precious gift— God invites us to come to him and ask him to work in our lives, and he promises to give us only good gifts in response to our prayers.

The Course of Your Life is built on these three gifts from God, and consists of three interconnected components or strands.

B. Three strands

i. Seminars

- Around 90 minutes in length.
- Addressing key topic areas by doing Bible research together, pulling ideas together, and praying together.
- There are nine seminars (including this opening one).

ii. One-to-one meetings

- With one other person, to read and pray together.
- Focusing on Paul's letter to the Colossians.
- Complementing and supporting the topics covered in the seminars.
- Providing opportunity to talk privately about what you're learning and being challenged by.

iii. Intensive

- Towards the end of the course (usually between seminars 8 and 9).
- Can be two days away together, or over consecutive Saturdays, or similar.
- Integrating and completing the course content.
- Providing time and space to think through the implications for different aspects of your own lives, and to pray.

The course has been designed so that these three strands interconnect and reinforce each other. The passages you study in your one-to-one meetings will feed into the seminar discussions, and the intensive will draw upon all the material that has been done in the one-to-one meetings and the seminars.

All this will take time and require a little patience. We won't answer every question by the end of seminar 3. If at various points in the course you feel a little frustrated, or even confused, that's not altogether a bad thing! A serious rethinking of our lives is not the easiest thing in the world to do. In God's grace, by the end of the course we hope and trust that you will have reached a new clarity.

4. More about the one-to-one meetings

For some of you, this may be the first time you've ever read the Bible one-to-one. Don't worry—it's not very difficult! And to make it even easier, we've provided you with a simple framework to use each time. This basically consists of:

- having a quick catch-up about what is happening in your life
- praying and giving thanks together briefly

- reading and discussing the Bible together for about 30 minutes (using the provided template/material)
- praying to conclude.

[At this point, you can flick over to the 'One-to-one meetings' section in the workbook and check out the template for the first one-to-one meeting.]

By far the most difficult thing about meeting one-to-one to read the Bible is… actually meeting. This is like Bible reading in general. The hardest aspect of personal Bible reading is usually just being disciplined enough to sit down, open the Bible and start reading. It's the same with meeting one-to-one. Working out a convenient time and then sticking to it—that's the key.

Once you're there it's really not that hard, and almost always very rewarding.

To make the meetings as convenient as possible, your course leader has tried to pair you up with someone who either lives or works close to you.

5. Meet your one-to-one partner

Apart from making a start on some Bible content, the aim of this section is for the one-to-one partners to get to know each other a little, and thus make their first meeting a little easier.

Divide everyone up into the pairs that you have already allocated, and work through the material below.

Timing: 30 minutes

A. Start by working out a suitable time and place for your first meeting—which needs to happen before seminar 2. (This might turn into your regular meeting time. You can sort that out when you get together.)

B. Share a little bit about yourself with your partner by answering one of the following questions:
- When you were 18 (which might have been 3 or 30 years ago!), did you have any dreams or goals in life? Have they been met?
- Can you think of a major mistake you have made in your life? What were the consequences?
- Think back to a reasonably major life decision you have made in the last five years (relating to work, family, friends, church, etc.). What were the key factors that determined your decision? What process did you go through in making up your mind?

C. Read Psalm 139:1-16 aloud together.

(i) What does this passage say about God's place in the course of our lives?

(ii) How does the psalmist feel about this? How does he react?

(iii) How do you react?

Finishing up

Depending on timing, you can conclude the seminar in these one-to-one pairings, or get back together in the whole group and share some answers/responses to the Psalm 139 questions. Pray to finish.

Timing: 20 minutes

God's creative purposes

About this seminar

In this seminar, we dive into the Bible and make a real start. And we start with the character of God as the sovereign creator and ruler of all things. There are two main reasons for this emphasis.

The first is theological: God's sovereignty as the creator and sustainer and ruler of all is the theological starting point for considering what our lives are about. We are creatures. We live in a ruled world. We do not create ourselves or fashion our own purpose for life. We are contingent. This lays the groundwork for arguing that it is God who determines the course of our lives, not us.

The second reason for starting at this point is to begin to unsettle the participants, and stretch their minds. The main spiritual problem we all have in working out what our lives are about and what they are for is our fundamental self-absorption. We find it hard to believe that life is not about Me and My happiness, satisfaction, fulfilment and pleasure (or at least about My family's enjoyment of all those things). The Copernican revolution that needs to take place in our thinking (i.e. that we are not at the centre of the universe, but God is)—begins with an understanding of God's supreme sovereignty as the creator.

You may wish to start this seminar with a brief discussion together, asking for feedback about how the first lot of one-to-one meetings went.

You can then outline the shape of this seminar, which starts with people in subgroups and finishes with everyone coming back together to share answers.

You will need large sheets of paper for each group to write on (and pens).

1. Bible research: God and his world

Do this section in two or more subgroups, working through the passages and noting basic content about God and his relation to our world. Divide the passages in part B up among the groups so that each passage is covered. If you have only one group then look at the following passages: Psalm 8, Psalm 135:5-7, Proverbs 19:21, Isaiah 45:1-9, Matthew 10:28-30 and Revelation 4:11.

Timing: 40 minutes

A. In your subgroups, read Genesis 1-2. As you read, think about the following two questions:

(i) Why did God make the world? What clues do we get here about his purposes or intentions?

(ii) More specifically, why did he make humanity? What purposes did he have in mind?

Spend a few minutes discussing your answers to these two questions.

B. Divide the following passages among the groups and fill in the table described below (you'll need to draw a larger version on the sheets of paper provided by your course leader). Select from:

Isaiah 14:24-27	Psalm 33
Isaiah 45:5-10	Proverbs 16:4
Isaiah 46:8-11	Acts 17:24-27
Isaiah 55:6-11	Revelation 4:11
Psalm 8	

As you do this exercise:
- Look up each passage as a group, and read it aloud.
- Choose one person to be the scribe.
- When questions arise, jot them in the 'question' column, but don't pause to discuss them (at this point).

- You won't be able to put things in every column for each passage.
- Keep moving quickly, and allow 5-10 minutes at the end of the exercise to do part C.

Draw up a table as follows. In each column jot down quickly what you learn about that subject in the Bible passages you have selected.

Passage	What do we learn about God the creator?	What do we learn about God's purposes or intentions?	What do we learn about ourselves?	Other notes and questions

C. Still in your subgroups, try to summarize the most important points you've picked up from your Bible research under the following headings:

(i) What did you learn about God the creator?

(ii) What did you learn about God's purposes or intentions for his creation?

(iii) What did you learn about yourself?

(iv) What questions puzzled you most?

2. Group feedback

Get one person from each group to share the group's findings/summaries. As they share their results, don't be afraid to interact with what they say—for example, to get them to clarify or push further.

If they share a question (from the last column in the table), throw it open for discussion among the whole group.

Timing: 25 minutes

3. Input: Who are we?

Play video clip 2 here, or give your own talk based on its content.

Timing: 10 minutes

Script:

I made this little man the other day. I used some play dough. I haven't quite decided what I will do with him. I might stick him on top of my computer monitor to remind me of writing this course. Or I might just throw him away. But whatever I do with him, it's pretty much up to me. I made him. He belongs to me. Whether he continues to exist is up to me. What purposes he serves are my decision—not his. Which is just as well, because he's not really up to making decisions.

But the thing is: he is my little creature, which I made for a particular purpose—to use in this video.

If we gain nothing else from reading Genesis 1 and 2, and from the other passages we've looked at in this seminar, at the very least we learn that we are God's creatures—in our case, animate, thinking, willing, living, breathing creatures, but creatures all the same.

We are not self-generated, nor did we simply pop into existence by chance. We are the creation of the God who made all things and who rules all things. In the words of Genesis 2, God fashioned us out of the dust of the earth and breathed life into our nostrils. He is the potter; we are the clay.

What's more, the God who brought us into existence is a rational, purposeful, intentional God. He doesn't make us for no reason. He works very intentionally. We see that clearly in Genesis 1, where God very deliberately creates every part of the world in order, and fills it with creatures, culminating in the creation of humanity. And God gives humanity a particular role: to be fruitful and multiply, to fill the earth and subdue it, to have dominion over all other living things.

The God who made us is a purposeful, intentional God. You no doubt also saw this in the various other passages you looked up. God has plans and intentions for his world, and he sees them through. God continues to rule and govern our world, to be completely in charge of its daily operation, to pursue his purposes within it. He didn't wind up our world like a clock and set it running, and then go off and get on with something else he had to do. God continues to be the sovereign, mighty ruler of every aspect of our world, including us—his creatures.

No purpose of this God can be thwarted or frustrated; nor can it even be questioned. It is not our place as the clay to tell the potter what he should be doing with what he has made.

Several implications flow from this. The first and most obvious is that we should honour and give thanks to this God who made us and owns us and rules us. He is worthy to receive glory and honour and power because he made all things (says Revelation 4:11). We need to recognize that God is God and we are not. Our lives are in his hands; we are dependent upon him for everything, including life and breath itself.

But God our maker not only determines **that** we exist; he also determines **why** we exist. As we think about the course of our lives—about what our lives are really for and where they are heading—this is a foundational truth: we don't determine the purpose and nature of our lives. God does.

We don't get to write our own mission statement. It simply is not our right. Our reason for existing is not self-derived or self-determined. It comes from outside of us—from the God who made us and who has his own purposes and intentions for us.

What are those purposes and intentions? Well, so far we've only seen them in broad outline. The first few pages of Genesis lay some foundations for understanding why God made humanity. He made us to live and multiply in his good world, and to rule over the other living creatures in the world. But there is much more to be said. The other 998 pages of the Bible build on the foundations of Genesis, and it is only when we get to Jesus and his place in God's great plans for the world that the whole picture really becomes clear. And we will come to this in the seminars to come.

But in the meantime, we need to pause and recognize just how much we hate the basic ideas that have come out in this seminar. Our lives are not our own to do with as we wish? We are like clay in the hands of a potter? Our dreams and desires and wishes in life should all be subordinated to Someone Else—to God?

These ideas grate against everything we hold dear. A thousand Disney movies have taught us that you should be free to follow your heart; that no-one else can tell you what is important in your life; that you need to discover that 'truth within'; that you need to find your dream and then follow it to the end of the rainbow.

There are very few basic beliefs that everyone in Western society shares, but this is one of them: the absolute right to self-determination; to be able to decide the course of our own lives, to be who we want to be, and not to let anyone else tell us who we are or what we have to do. The prominence of this idea in our world—the pursuit of personal freedom and autonomy as the highest goal of life—has a long history, and we don't have time to trace that history now. But it is in the air we breathe, the TV shows and movies we watch, the books we read, the education system we are raised in.

Now as Christians, we know there is something wrong with this idea. We acknowledge that God really is God, and that we should submit to his plans—not our own. But we often underestimate just how deeply and stubbornly we also believe in self-determination, in basically charting our own course in life. But doing things our own way, and determining our own course in life, comes very naturally to us.

This is revealed not only in how little thanks we give to God our creator for everything he gives us, but also in how rarely we pause to consider his purposes and intentions for us as we make decisions about our lives.

We would much prefer to be in the position of the potter rather than the clay. And this desire and its consequences (as we will see in our next seminar) are as old as humanity itself.

4. Discussion and prayer

Give participants the opportunity for discussion, questions and comments on the input. Don't be concerned if you can't answer everything—in fact, having some unanswered questions at this point in the course is probably a good thing.

Leave some time at the end for a few people to close in prayer.

Timing: 10-15 minutes

Seminar 3
What went wrong?

About this seminar

In this seminar, we examine the consequences of sin and the Fall, and the implications for the course of our lives. We start with Genesis 2-3 and the sin of Adam and Eve, considering not only the nature of their rebellion (to distrust God's goodness and rebel against his God-ness) but also its punishment (death, decay, frustration). What we see in embryo and outline in Genesis 3 is worked out in more detail as the Bible unfolds.

The Bible research element of this seminar focuses on the part of the Bible that, more than any other, probes the grim realities of life in a post-Eden world: Ecclesiastes.

One of the key lessons in this seminar is realizing that we can't control our life, or really know its course; and that many of our treasured dreams and ambitions are rendered foolish and absurd by the nature of life in our fallen world.

1. Input: What went wrong?

Play video clip 3 here, or give your own talk based on its content. This input summarizes where we're up to, describes the main teaching of Genesis 2-3, and lays the groundwork for the subsequent Bible research in Ecclesiastes.

Timing: 10 minutes

Script:

Most great dramas start with an establishing scene. The camera pans across a charming garden to a cottage, and in through the kitchen window you see a young family having breakfast together. Peaceful music plays in the background. Dad is getting ready for work. He engages in some friendly banter with his son, who is at the table. His loving wife, who has everything under control, kisses him goodbye.

And you know—you just **know**—that very shortly it's all going to come unstuck. Some tragedy will strike: a robbery; a murder; an infidelity; an earthquake; an alien invasion. Something will break the idyllic picture to pieces, and the rest of the story will be about trying to put it back together again.

Perhaps we resonate with those sorts of opening scenes because it is also **our** opening scene. The human drama starts the same way. As we saw in seminar 2, God creates a good world—a very good world—in which he puts mankind; and it is clear that he has certain plans and purposes for his creation. It is a beautiful and idyllic picture, although that doesn't mean it is a finished picture. You don't get the sense in Genesis 1 and 2 that the story is over. It is just beginning. God tells humanity to fill the earth and subdue it, and to have dominion over all its creatures. There is a destiny for humanity in God's plans.

But before almost any of that can happen, it all comes unstuck. Eve listens to one of the crawling things over which she is supposed to have dominion, and as a result comes to doubt the goodness of God's intentions. Does God really have her best interests at heart? Does he really want good for her, or is he trying to stop her from reaching her potential? She decides that she knows better than God, and eats of the tree; and her idiot of a husband, Adam, obediently does the same.

What is the essence of Adam and Eve's sin? It is not just a lack of trust in God's goodness, but also an unwillingness to recognize God's God-ness—that he is the good creator who is in charge. Adam and Eve rebel against God and his rule; they flout his clear commands; they wish to become like God themselves. They make a fateful play for control, for being able to chart their own purpose and destiny in life.

But God remains God, and humanity's grab for power is doomed to failure. And so Adam and Eve are judged and punished.

The punishment is dreadful. It not only brings death and decay into their lives, but also strikes at the heart of their task of being fruitful and multiplying and subduing the earth. Childbirth will be painful; there will be conflict in the marriage relationship; there will be conflict with the animal kingdom; and the very ground itself will become unyielding and hostile.

It all seems to have gone so wrong. The destiny and purpose God had for mankind seems to have been derailed almost as soon as he created us.

This is the world we now live in: a world marred by death and decay, by relational conflict, and by struggle, pain, suffering and difficulty; a world where humanity seems able to do and achieve so much that is good, but in the next breath do and achieve so much that is evil.

In Genesis, we see all of this in embryo form. We see the basic problem: humanity's stupid sinful rebellion against our creator and Lord. And we see the basic consequences: death and decay, suffering and pain, conflict and hardship.

This has very obvious implications for the course of our lives; for understanding what we are like, what we are for, and where we are headed. For a start, and most obviously, it means that the course of our lives will come to an end; we will return to dust. And it means that all the plans and dreams and hopes we might have had in this world will dissolve into dust as well.

But it also means that the path we tread between birth and death will be a difficult one in terms of our relationships and our work. The course of our lives won't be a smooth path of rose petals and sunshine. It will be rocky, painful, frustrating and difficult.

All this is foreshadowed and outlined in Genesis 1-3. And as the revelation of the Bible unfolds, this outline is filled out. We see more clearly and in more detail the nature of our sinfulness and rebellion; the nature of the consequences; and the nature of the implications—what it means for our daily lives, for our purpose in life, and for our future.

Before we go too much further in considering our lives and what they are for and where we are heading, we need to come to grips with the grim realities of what life is really like in our post-Eden world.

That's what we'll be doing in this seminar. And we'll do so by looking at a part of the Bible that deals with this issue most starkly: the book of Ecclesiastes.

2. Bible research: The grim realities

Divide into at least two subgroups for this exercise. Allocate Ecclesiastes 3 to one group and Ecclesiastes 8:16-9:12 to the other.

Timing: 25 minutes

A. Read Ecclesiastes 3.

(i) What does this passage teach us about life?

(ii) What do we know and understand?

(iii) What do we **not** know and understand?

(iv) Why has God put us in this situation?

(v) What is the factor that renders all our striving a bit meaningless?

(vi) So what does the Preacher recommend in the circumstances?

(vii) If you were going to use Ecclesiastes 3 to give a nugget of wise advice about life to a child, what would it be?

B. Read Ecclesiastes 8:16-9:12.

(i) What does this passage teach us about life?

(ii) What is the state of humanity's heart?

(iii) What can we **not** know or figure out?

(iv) What event frustrates our attempt to understand and to control our lives?

(v) What conclusions does the Preacher draw from this?

(vi) If you were going to use this passage to give a nugget of wise advice about life to a child, what would it be?

3. Group feedback

Get each group to share what they have learned. Discuss and ask questions.

Timing: 20 minutes

4. Input: Where to turn?

Play video clip 4 here, or give your own talk based on its content.

Timing: 15 minutes

Script:

Maybe it's because of the classic 60s folk song 'Turn, turn, turn', but Ecclesiastes 3 is one of the best-known chapters in the Bible. For everything there is a season, and a time for every purpose under heaven; a time to be born and a time to die; a time for this and a time for that.

This is the picture of the world that the book of Ecclesiastes keeps painting for us—with all its ceaseless to-ing and fro-ing: a generation comes and a generation goes; the sun comes up and goes back down; the wind blows to the south and then to the north and then back again; what has been will be again, and what has been done will be done again. The world just seems to go round and round, on and on, getting nowhere.

And this is true of human life as well. There is a time for everything, and for its opposite. Sometimes we plant; sometimes we have to pluck up what is planted. Sometimes we weep; sometimes we laugh. There is even a time for war, just as there is a time for peace.

Everything seems to have its time, and to fit in its time. In fact, in Ecclesiastes 3:11, the writer says that God "has made everything beautiful in its time". And we can sense that this is true—that there is a God at work in our world, who lives in eternity and gives meaning and significance to human life. We sense that there is a larger purpose, a larger framework, in which everything that happens in the world fits.

I think this is what the author of Ecclesiastes means when he says that God has put eternity into man's heart. We know there is more to life than just one thing happening randomly after another. And yet... even though we sense this larger picture, and that there is a God at work in our world, we cannot discover what he is doing or fathom his purpose. We sense there is purpose and meaning to the course of our lives—or that there should be—but it eludes us. It escapes us.

This can be frustrating, and humbling. But not nearly as humbling as what the writer goes on to say in Ecclesiastes 3—which is that the unavoidable reality of death casts a mocking shadow over all our pretensions.

> I said in my heart with regard to the children of man that God is testing them that they may see that they themselves are but beasts. [19] For what happens to the children of man and what happens to the beasts is the same; as one dies, so dies the other. They all have the same breath, and man has no advantage over the beasts, for all is vanity. [20] All go to one place. All are from the dust, and to dust all return. (Eccl 3:18-20)

The writer takes us back to the garden, where man and beast are both formed from the dust of the earth, and have God's breath breathed into their nostrils. And he reminds us of the awful judgement that has fallen on humanity. We have been cast out of the garden and denied any further access to the tree of life that stood at its centre. So now we must die and return to the dust, just like the beasts.

Death is the one terrible fate that awaits all creatures. And it pricks the bubble of human pride and self-regard. We make such grand plans, and think that we will achieve such great things. Some of us even do achieve great things, and build houses for ourselves and live in comfort and security—as Solomon does in Ecclesiastes. But death awaits us we know not when; and in the face of death, all our plans and dreams and achievements are about as significant as the plans and dreams of a cow.

James says much the same thing in the New Testament:

Come now, you who say, "Today or tomorrow we will go into such and such a town and spend a year there and trade and make a profit"—[14] yet you do not know what tomorrow will bring. What is your life? For you are a mist that appears for a little time and then vanishes. [15] Instead you ought to say, "If the Lord wills, we will live and do this or that." [16] As it is, you boast in your arrogance. All such boasting is evil. (Jas 4:13-16)

We need to feel the weight of this if we are going to understand the course of our lives. We need to honestly face just how fickle, frustrating and unpredictable human life can be—not to mention wicked and unjust. The passage we studied in Ecclesiastes 8 and 9 makes this point very forcefully. There is not just eternity in man's heart, but evil and madness as well. We do unspeakable things to each other.

And yet the wicked man perishes and returns to dust, just like the righteous man.

This is the world we live in: a rebel planet under God's judgement, where death and decay and injustice are our common experience. Now, it's still a good world. And God still gives us good things to enjoy—in fact, the writer of Ecclesiastes recommends that we might as well enjoy them while we can, because we don't know what's around the corner.

But we need to repent of the foolish dream that we can actually control our lives, and bend the world to our will. Some of us know this already from bitter experience. Some of us might still be living in the fantasy that we are in control, that we can chart our own destiny and make all our dreams come true.

Before we can hear God's answer to the frustration, evil, injustice and death that scar our lives, we must repent of thinking we can master them ourselves. We need to turn back to God, and humbly listen to the answer **he** gives to the frustration of our lives.

And it is to the beginnings of this answer that we will turn in our next seminar.

5. Discussion and prayer

Give participants the opportunity for discussion, questions and comments on the input. If the conversation is slow to get going, you might like to pose some questions like these:

- Which aspects of Ecclesiastes ring especially true for you in your experience?
- When do you feel most in control of life? Least in control?

Leave some time at the end for a few people to close in prayer.

Timing: 10-15 minutes

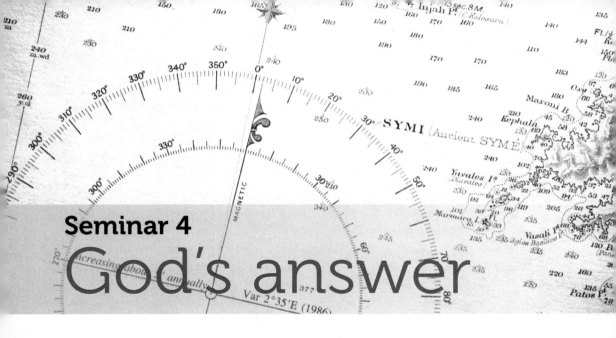

Seminar 4
God's answer

About this seminar

This seminar is really about the sufficiency of Scripture—the idea that God's revealed answer to the problems that beset us is not only true and authoritative, but also sufficient. We don't need anything else. In fact, God's answer helps us to understand what the question really was.

This is a very important seminar in establishing that God has a purpose or agenda for our world and for each one of us, and that this agenda is not something that we can just slip into our existing busy agenda.

1. Input: God's answer

Play video clip 5 here, or give your own talk based on its content.

Timing: 7 minutes

Script:

Sometimes bad news is actually good news—for example, when you've had a nagging health problem that has dragged on for months, and the doctor finally figures out what's wrong with you. Even though it's bad news (you've got this particular disease), in another sense it's good news because at least now you can start treating the problem.

The dismal point we reached at the end of our last seminar is a bit like that.

So far, we have seen that God purposefully created a good and beautiful world, with humanity being the pinnacle of his creation, given the joyous responsibility of filling and subduing the world, of having dominion over it under God.

And yet the sin of humanity, and God's judgement on it, seem to have derailed God's purposes: that is, death and decay are universal, injustice and wickedness are everywhere, and bad things happen to people seemingly without rhyme or reason. All in all we don't really know where we're going, what life is about, or what it is that really distinguishes us from the beasts, since—like them—we will return to dust, and all of our dreams and achievements will likewise turn to dust.

In the face of this dismal and frustrating situation, the best we can do is enjoy the moment, if we happen to be blessed with that possibility.

This vision of life from Ecclesiastes is very like the vision that most of our neighbours and friends share: that is, there are good things in life worth enjoying (food, work, family, leisure, and so on). But life is also so chaotic, unpredictable and (often) awful, that there is no point trying to come up with a grand scheme or design. We don't really know what God is like or what life is about, so we might as well live for the moment, or the few moments ahead.

But, as the writer of Ecclesiastes points out, this makes us little different from the beasts, who also live for the next mouthful of grass they will chew, and like us return to the dust when they die.

Now if the story stops here, it would be like the doctor giving us the bad news, "You have a very serious illness" and then saying, "And by the way, there is no cure".

But thanks be to God, the story doesn't stop there. The whole Bible is the story of God's answer to the problem, if we can put it like that.

And his answer is not just information: that is like the answer to a riddle. His answer is also an action, like the answer to the problem of a disease (which is to provide a cure). In fact, as we will begin to see in this seminar, God's answer is even more than information and even more than an action.

But beware: God's answer will completely change the course of your life. If it is true, then it defines our world and our reality.

So proceed with caution.

2. Bible research: Knowledge of God and where to find it

If you have less than ten group members, do this study as one group. If your group is larger than this, divide into subgroups of five or so. Each group should look at all three passages.

Timing: 35 minutes

A. Read Psalm 19.

(i) How does God reveal himself?

(ii) What sort of knowledge of God is revealed in creation?

(iii) What should be our response to it?

(iv) What sort of knowledge is revealed in the law of the Lord?

(v) What should be our response to it?

B. Read Hebrews 1:1-4.

(i) How and when has God spoken in the past?

(ii) How has God spoken more recently?

(iii) What do you think "in these last days" means?

(iv) What else do we learn about the word that God has spoken in these last days?

C. Read 2 Peter 1:1-4.

(i) What has God given us?

(ii) Through what (or whom) has he given us this?

(iii) What is the end point or goal?

3. Input: God's sufficient word

Play video clip 6 here, or give your own talk based on its content.

Timing: 15 minutes

Script:

A. God's sufficient word

Growing as a Christian consists in large measure of coming to realize how momentous and world-altering is the decision to become a Christian. It gradually dawns on us, often over a period of many years, what a radical step we've taken. We come to realize that what we have held in our hands all this time is bigger and more explosive than we had ever thought.

Case in point: the Bible. We believe it is God's book; that it is his word; that it is inspired and true. If you don't believe that then you can hardly be a Christian, since the only source of knowledge we have for who Jesus really is and what the whole show is about is in the words that have been written down and preserved in this book. If the book is untrue or unreliable then all that we believe is untrue or unreliable.

So to become a Christian is to believe in the truth of the Bible—almost unavoidably. Of all the many Christian people I've met and talked to over the past 30 years, I can't remember even one of them who openly disparaged or discredited the Bible.

But we don't always appreciate just how radical it is to believe the Bible.

For if we believe what the Bible says about itself, then this is no ordinary book. It claims to be the breathed-out word of a sovereign mighty creator God, who sustains and upholds and rules all things—a God who has revealed himself and spoken through prophets, through his law, and finally and majestically by his own Son.

And this climactic revelation through his Son is not some peripheral subject, but concerns the very nature of reality in this world—such as who God really is, who rules this world, who we are as God's creatures, what our lives are about, what the purpose of the universe is, what constitutes the truly good life, how we can be forgiven and reconciled with God. All this is finally revealed and made clear through Jesus.

This is what you are saying you believe if you believe the Bible—because this is what the Bible says about itself. You should have picked that up as you studied Psalm 19, Hebrews 1 and 2 Peter 1.

Now this belief carries with it a momentous implication. If this is the nature of God's revelation, then that revelation is not only true and reliable—it is also **sufficient**. God's revelation in Scripture tells us all we need to know. We do not need any extra information in order to live in this world in the way God intended. This is the message of 2 Peter 1: through the knowledge of Jesus that comes by his word, we have all we need for life and godliness.

But this belief implies something else as well. If God's revelation tells us all the truly important things we need to know for the course of our lives, then it also tells us which questions are really important, which issues are really crucial, which variables in our lives are the really critical ones. It means that the Bible not only tells us the truth about matters, but also tells us which matters really matter.

B. God's agenda

So how does this help us in understanding the course of our lives, and in making decisions?

I'm about to give you an illustration so graphic and so horrifying, that unless you are mentally prepared for the shock, you may not recover for several days.

Are you ready?

I want you to imagine that your life is a committee meeting—one incredibly long meeting in a slightly stuffy room with fluorescent lighting and uncomfortable chairs. The shuffling into the room is your birth, the interminable proceedings in the middle are what pass for your daily life, and the blank-eyed, desultory dispersal at the end is the whimper with which your life ends.

I apologize for lodging that image in your mind, but I do it for good reason. I want you to ponder a very important question: if your life was a committee meeting (perish the thought), what would the **agenda** of the meeting be?

Because all meetings have an agenda. Sometimes it's unspoken or haphazard. But in a better sort of meeting, it's actually written down and carefully structured with the most important items and topics at the top, so that there's plenty of time to discuss them and make decisions.

So what about the committee meeting of your life? What sort of agenda does it have? It does have one, although you probably don't ever write it down or even consciously think about it. But it is there. You have a mental list of the important things to be done in your life, in order of priority.

So if you were to be honest and write down the half-dozen or so things that are most important to you, and which dictate your daily and weekly routine, what would they be?

If you're a typical young woman in your early twenties, your agenda might be something this:

1. Find a job that will kick-start my career.
2. Save enough to travel.
3. Find a boyfriend.
4. Fill my life with memorable experiences.

Or if you're a married middle-aged man, perhaps your unspoken life agenda is more like this:

1. Keep wife happy (because happy wife = happy life).
2. Get the kids into good schools.
3. Buy best house in best suburb I can afford.
4. Earn enough money to do 1-3 in a job that doesn't frustrate me to death.
5. Have some fun, although 1-4 will probably prevent that happening.

Now life agendas like these are based on the assumption that the overriding purpose of your life is to be happy, successful and fulfilled.

And if that's your purpose, and these are your real priorities in life, then you'll make decisions and take action accordingly. These items will dominate your thinking. They will be the matters that really matter.

But what happens when we become Christians? How does that affect the agenda of our life?

People have strange ideas about this.

Some people think, for example, that being a Christian is like having God as one of your co-workers so that you get through your agenda really successfully and well. Becoming a Christian doesn't change your life agenda—it just makes it easier to achieve because you have God on your side!

This is pretty self-centred and a bit arrogant as well—as if we know better than our creator what is important and worth achieving in life! But it's a very common mindset, especially among Christians who haven't really grasped what a radical thing it is to submit to Christ.

Other people think that becoming a Christian, or getting more involved in church, is really about adding something to my agenda—perhaps something that was missing: the spiritual side of life that will make me a more rounded individual. It's a bit like one of those important subjects you know you should get to in the meeting, but which always somehow falls down the list because of the business arising. And so there is a new agenda item called 'Be involved in Christ and church-type stuff'. And you see it as your aim to try to move it up the agenda a bit more.

In fact, you might even think that the aim of **this course** is to get you to move the Christ and church stuff further up your agenda.

Not so.

If what we have been saying about God's revelation is true, then what he has revealed to us about the world and about his Son is not something we put on our agenda. He is not something that we try to fit in; he is not one of the balls that we are trying to juggle. If what we have been saying about God's revelation is true, then what he has revealed to us about the world and about his Son doesn't add to our agenda. **Can you see that it *completely rewrites* our agenda? It screws up the piece of paper that our little list of ambitions and priorities is written on, and replaces it with a fresh sheet of paper and a completely fresh agenda.**

Now the question is: what is on that fresh sheet of paper? What is God's new agenda for the course of our lives?

And that's what we'll start discussing in our next seminar.

4. Discussion and prayer: What does this mean for us?

Talk together about what it means for God's word to be sufficient, and for it to set our agenda. What questions does it raise?

Finish by praying together in pairs or triplets.

Timing: 15 minutes

Seminar 5
God's agenda

About this seminar

We've come to the point in the course where we start laying out what God's purposes and intentions are for our lives—what we will call God's **agenda** for the world and for our lives.

In essence, God's agenda is revealed in the gospel, so this seminar focuses on some classic New Testament passages that outline how God's purposes for our world are revealed in Christ.

This is a 'big picture' summary. In the seminars to come, we will zero in on the specifics of how God's agenda connects with our lives.

1. The story so far

Give your own summary of where we have come to, using the points below.

Timing: 5 minutes

What have we learned so far in *The Course of Your Life*?

A. In seminar 2, we saw that to understand ourselves and our lives, we need to start with creation, for we are all creatures of the one good and sovereign God. God is the potter, we are the clay, and he made us intentionally and deliberately. He had purposes for humanity, and they are outlined in Genesis: to be fruitful and multiply, to fill the earth and subdue it, to have dominion over all other living things.

So the rationale for our lives—for who we are, and why we are on this planet—is not self-generated. We don't impart meaning to our own lives. God our creator writes our mission statement and determines the course of our lives. And this grates against many of our deepest and most basic Western beliefs.

B. In seminar 3, we looked at how it all seemed to go wrong.

We don't like bowing to God's God-ness. Adam and Eve didn't like it, and so they rebelled and were judged. They decided to write their own rules—to break God's rule—so they were judged and cast out. This is now who we are: rebels under judgement, excluded/alienated from God and his purposes, and under the reign of decay and death.

What does this mean for God's purposes? They seem to be frustrated. God's plan seems to have gone off the rails almost as soon as it got under way.

What does it mean for us and for our lives? The world we live in and the course of our lives looks like Ecclesiastes. We sense meaning. But we can't grasp it, and it all seems absurd. We felt some of the weight of this: the frustration and unpredictability of human life; the universality of injustice, evil and death; the foolishness of thinking that we can sort out our own lives and control them.

C. But then last time, in seminar 4, we saw that God has an answer to the death, decay and absurdity of the fallen world and our lives. God's purposes are not frustrated. God's answer is revealed first in the Old Testament and then finally and majestically through his Son (Heb 1:1-4).

If God's answer to sin and evil and death is found in the Scriptural revelation culminating in Jesus, then this has radical implications for how we think about our lives. What God says is not an additional item to be fitted into the busy agenda of our lives. Instead, it completely rewrites the agenda of our lives.

D. And so now we need to ask: Well, what is God's agenda? What's the plan? What is God really doing and focusing on in our world?

And we're going to do this by working together on four magnificent New Testament passages that summarize God's agenda for the world and for our lives.

2. Bible research: What is God's agenda?

To cover all four passages in this exercise, divide your group into four subgroups (it doesn't matter if each group is only a pair or a triplet). If you are still short of numbers, skip the Titus passage.

Timing: 25 minutes

Choose one of the following four passages and read it through a couple of times. Your goal in this exercise is to summarize in a paragraph or so what this passage tells you about God's agenda. What is God doing in the world? What is he focused on? What is his plan for the world and for us?

A. Acts 17:22-31

Questions that might help you:

- What is Paul's argument against idols and human religion?
- What does this passage say about how the world came to be the way it is? Was there a purpose to it being this way?
- If you were going to write a very short history of the world (in about four sentences) from this passage, what would it be?
- What part does Jesus play in this history?

Your summary of God's agenda:

B. Ephesians 1:1-10

Questions that might help you:

- Look for all the times Paul uses the phrase "in Christ" or "in him". What has God done in Christ?
- What's the timeline of this passage? When does it date from? And when does it go to?
- What is God's ultimate goal or purpose across all this span of time?
- When did this plan finally become known?

Your summary of God's agenda:

C. Colossians 1:1-20

Questions that might help you:

- In verses 3-6, the gospel almost has a life of its own. What is the gospel doing?
- What had the gospel done or produced in the Colossians' lives?
- What does Paul hope and pray they will continue in/grow in?
- Who is the Son? What is his place in God's plans?

Your summary of God's agenda:

D. Titus 2:11-14

Questions that might help you:

- What has happened in the past?
- What will happen in the future?
- What should happen in the meantime?
- What was the ultimate plan of "our great God and Saviour Jesus Christ"?

Your summary of God's agenda:

3. Group feedback

Get each group to share what they have learned about God's agenda for our world and for our lives. Discuss and ask questions.

Timing: 25 minutes

4. Input: The secret of life

Play video clip 7 here, or give your own talk based on its content.

Timing: 15 minutes

Script:

So far in this seminar, we've read and studied some of the most profound passages in the Bible—passages that talk about God's purposes for the whole world and for our lives.

What do we learn as we put these amazing New Testament passages together?

A. We learn firstly that God's agenda or purpose is not just about me but about all of history and all of the world (all time and all nations).

We see this in the Acts 17 speech, which is the only one of our passages that was directed to outsiders. Paul explains to the curious Athenians that God's age-long plans for the entire world have finally come to fruition and have now been revealed. God has now set a date for the judgement of the world by Jesus Christ, has confirmed it by raising him from the dead, and now calls on all nations to turn back to him while they can.

God's purpose, announced in the gospel, is cosmic, worldwide, momentous.

It's not how we're used to thinking about it. We tend to think of the gospel as a personal message about me and my sin, and my own personal need to be saved and to live with Jesus as my Lord—which it is.

But in the New Testament, the personal appeal and relevance of the gospel message is based in the fact that it's momentous, earth-shattering news concerning the whole world and the whole of human history.

B. The second and intriguing thing we learn is that this momentous, earth-shattering purpose of God was largely hidden and secret until the gospel revelation of Jesus Christ. The gospel announcement is like the speech the detective makes in an Agatha Christie novel towards the end, where he finally reveals who the murderer is and how the tangled series of events all make sense once the final piece of the puzzle is revealed. God's plan was a mystery long hidden but now finally revealed.

The Old Testament foreshadowed it—the prophets predicted it, without fully understanding themselves when and how it would happen.

But now it has happened. The curtain has been thrown back and the mystery has now been made known at last, revealed to the entire world through the gospel of Jesus.

And what is the now-open secret? What is the "word of truth" that is now revealed?

It is that God has sent his Son Jesus into the world as a man to be the king and ruler of a new kingdom, to which redeemed and purified people from every nation (not just Israel) will belong. He has sent him to be the Christ (for that is what Christ means: God's chosen king), and to rule over a new kingdom of God—a new creation, where there is no sin or pain or suffering or decay or death.

C. You see, God's agenda addresses the basic problem of our world and of our lives: the alienation, the enmity, the sin, the suffering, the decay, the frustration and confusion. The kingdom of the Son will be nothing like this; it will be a new and perfect creation. And only the perfect will belong there—so our sin renders us ineligible for this new kingdom of God.

And this is why God's action in Christ was to come and cleanse and forgive and redeem sinful people: so that they could be citizens of his eternal kingdom.

Jesus comes not only to assume the throne as the king of God's kingdom, but also to deliver and save his people—because that's what kings and Christs do: they fight for their people, they rescue and deliver and redeem their people, they defeat their people's enemies and bring peace.

This is what Jesus did by dying and rising again. The cross and resurrection were the steps at the base of his throne. And by dying as a sacrifice for sin, he is able to deliver people out of darkness and transfer them into his kingdom. He is able to offer redemption and the forgiveness of sin.

Being transferred into his kingdom is a massive and radical change: a new citizenship, a new domain; from darkness to light. It means being a subject or citizen of the kingdom that is surely coming.

Can you see? God's agenda is actually about Jesus more than us! His agenda is to unite all things in Jesus, to deliver people into the kingdom of Jesus, to glorify Jesus, to purify a people for Jesus, to appoint Jesus as the king of the universe, and for people everywhere to acknowledge Jesus as Lord.

Summary: If we were going to visualize God's agenda in our world from what we have seen so far, we could use a simple diagram like this:

God's cosmic purpose, his plan, his priority, his agenda in this world is to transfer forgiven rebels like us out of the domain of darkness and into the kingdom of his Son.

And the key moment in God's agenda was the cross: the death and resurrection of Jesus. If we're going to understand God's plan, and especially how it relates to our lives, our plans, our desires and our dreams, then before we do anything else we need to dig a little deeper and understand the significance of Jesus' death and resurrection—which we'll do in our next seminar.

5. Discussion and prayer

Give participants the opportunity for discussion, questions and comments on the input. Leave some time at the end for a few people to close in prayer.

Timing: 15 minutes

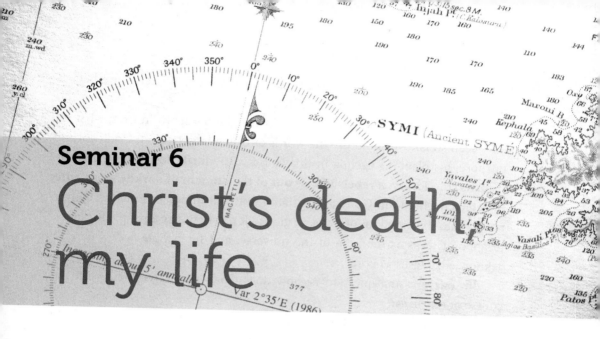

Seminar 6
Christ's death, my life

About this seminar

This seminar we focus in on where the big picture of what God is doing in the world connects with our own individual lives. And the point of connection is the cross of Christ. At the cross, Jesus makes it possible for sinful rebels to be delivered from darkness and transferred to his kingdom.

In particular, this seminar explains the representative nature of Jesus' death—that Jesus dies not only as our **substitute** (instead of us), but also as our **representative** (as us). By being united with Jesus in his death, our old lives of rebellion and darkness are put to death on the cross. We are crucified with Christ, and a whole new life begins.

So to understand the course of our lives, we need to understand that our old self has died, and that we have been born again to a new life through the death and resurrection of Jesus.

1. Input: Where are we up to?

Read through the summary text below with the group.

Timing: 5 minutes

We've seen that if God is the sovereign creator who has plans and intentions for this world, and if he has revealed these purposes in these last days by his Son, then what he has revealed in the Scriptures doesn't just add to my busy agenda—it rewrites it. The Bible reveals which matters matter. If we believe this, it will change the course of our lives.

If we were going to summarize God's agenda in our world from what we have seen so far, we could use the words of Colossians 1:13-14: God's cosmic purpose, his plan, his agenda in this world is **to glorify Jesus the Christ by transferring forgiven rebels like us out of the domain of darkness and into his eternal kingdom**. God's agenda is to unite all things in Jesus, to deliver people into the kingdom of Jesus, to glorify Jesus, to purify a people for Jesus, to appoint Jesus as the king of the universe, and for people everywhere to acknowledge Jesus as Lord.

But our pressing question is: how does God's agenda connect with the course of **our** lives?

And to understand that, we need to understand the key moment in God's unfolding plan: the death and resurrection of Jesus.

We need to take some time to understand it, because the death of Jesus is the point of intersection between God's agenda and our lives. It is through the death of Jesus that God's plan shapes the course of our lives.

2. Bible research: Explaining the cross

Read through this task with the whole group and then divide up into subgroups, allocating the passages among the groups.

Timing: 25 minutes

Imagine you invite a friend along to church one day, and they hear a talk that mentions Jesus' death. You're chatting afterwards, and when you ask them what they thought of the sermon, they say to you: "Well, to be honest, I don't really understand what all the fuss is about the crucifixion of Jesus. I can understand that he died, and that it was an act of sacrifice or something. But I can't really see what it's got to do with me and my life."

And then you say to them (in a moment of boldness and clarity), "Do you mind if I show you this passage I love in the Bible? It exactly answers your question about why Jesus' death is so important, and what it has to do with us and our lives."

Your Bible research exercise is to come up with an explanation from one of the following passages that would explain to your friend:

A. what Jesus' death really meant (i.e. what it achieved or why it was necessary)

B. what difference Jesus' death makes to us and to our lives (i.e. how it connects with us; how it affects us).

Romans 5:6-10
Colossians 2:11-15
1 Peter 2:22-25
2 Corinthians 5:17-21

A. What Jesus' death really meant:

B. What difference Jesus' death makes to us and to our lives:

3. Group feedback

Get each subgroup to share their explanation. As each does so, the rest of the group could pretend to be the non-Christian questioner, and ask follow-up questions.

Timing: 20 minutes

Share your presentations with one another.

4. Input: Christ's death and ours

Play video clip 8 here, or give your own talk based on its content. This is a slightly longer piece of input than usual.

Timing: 20 minutes

Script:

So far in this seminar, you've been studying different passages about the death of Jesus, and you've no doubt talked together about what it means for Jesus to die for us, to die as our **substitute**. Jesus died to bear our sins in his body on the tree, to take upon himself the penalty that we deserve—so that we can be justified and forgiven and redeemed and cleansed and reconciled to God.

This of course is the very heart of the gospel. It's the beating heart of the letter to the Colossians that we've been spending so much time in recently. Paul reminds the Colossians that they have been transferred from the domain of darkness and into the kingdom of his Son—and not by obeying the law, or by performing good works, or by abstaining from certain foods, or by doing religious rituals. They could be transferred from one domain to the other **only** because of the redemption won by Christ Jesus, the forgiveness of sins, the reconciliation he achieved by his death.

Or, as Paul puts it in his letter to the Romans: we are justified and saved and redeemed and declared righteous as a generous and free gift (Rom 3:23-24). It's not something that we earn. By our sin we earn and deserve judgement and death, but although the wages of sin is death, the free gift of God is eternal life through Jesus Christ our Lord (Rom 6:23).

These are sweet and amazing truths, and there is nothing better to fill our minds with.

But the free grace and mercy of the cross raises a question that is as old as Christianity. It's a question that Paul himself had to deal with in his letters. And the question is: if God has freely and completely forgiven me through the death and resurrection of Jesus—if it is all by grace and not by works—then what incentive is there for me to lead a new life of godliness and righteousness? In fact, if God's grace is the response and answer to our sinful rebellion, then why not sin all the more so that God's grace might also increase?

In other words, the cross is at the centre of God's plan for the world and for us. It secures our entry into the eternal kingdom of the Son. But once it has done that, how does it affect our daily lives?

This was a big question for the New Testament Christians. It's a big question today. For many Christians, Jesus' death and resurrection is like an entry ticket into heaven that you need to keep in your back pocket to ensure that you get in. But now that you have your entry ticket, does it **really** matter how you live? In fact, if you try too hard to be holy, wouldn't you be in danger of thinking that your 'good works' might make you acceptable to God?

Now we sense that this is not right, but we often find it hard to say why. Just how does the death and resurrection of Jesus shape and drive and motivate the course of our daily lives?

Well, the best place I know of to answer that question is in one of the most remarkable passages in the entire Bible.

In 2 Corinthians 5, the apostle Paul is explaining some of his motivations to the Corinthians, who are just a bit distrustful of him, it seems. So Paul opens his heart to them, and explains just why he does what he does—because Paul's life is pretty full-on. In fact, to the outside observer he almost seems a bit mad, like a religious fanatic. He seems to have no regard for his own safety, comfort or wellbeing. He works hard and constantly for the sake of gospel, and for the sake of the churches that the gospel has given birth to. He accepts and embraces danger, hardship, hunger, floggings, anxiety and mistreatment of all kinds for the sake of Jesus.

Ironically, Paul's rather extreme behaviour has led the Corinthians to doubt him, to just pull back from him a touch. So in this letter, Paul is explaining himself and seeking to win the Corinthians' trust and affection. And in chapter 5 he explains just what motivates and drives this life he leads. Starting at verse 11 he says:

> Therefore, knowing the fear of the Lord, we persuade others. But what we are is known to God, and I hope it is known also to your conscience. [12] We are not commending ourselves to you again but giving you cause to boast about us, so that you may be able to answer those who boast about outward appearance and not about what is in the heart. [13] For if we are beside ourselves, it is for God; if we are in our right mind, it is for you. [14] For the love of Christ controls us, because we have concluded this: that one has died for all, therefore all have died; [15] and he died for all, that those who live might no longer live for themselves but for him who for their sake died and was raised.
>
> [16] From now on, therefore, we regard no-one according to the flesh. Even though we once regarded Christ according to the flesh, we regard him thus no longer. [17] Therefore, if anyone is in Christ, he is a new creation. The old has passed away; behold, the new has come. (2 Cor 5:11-17)

Did you notice Paul's explanation for why he lives the way he does?

It's because he has no choice. **The love of Christ controls or compels him** (in verse 14) to think and speak and live the way he does.

To be 'controlled' means to be hemmed in, to be left with no other options, to be driven down a certain path because there is no way back, and there are two high walls on each side.

And what controls Paul and gives him no choice is the love of Christ, and particularly the love of Christ in his death on the cross.

Now by saying that the love of Christ controls him, Paul doesn't mean that it sets him an example. It's not that Paul looks at the love of Christ for him and is moved in his heart by it. It's not that Christ is inspirational. Christ is of course an inspirational example, but it's not inspiration or example that is driving Paul.

He's also not speaking about gratitude. It's not that Paul is so thankful for the free gift that Christ has given him on the cross that he wants to lead a new life out of gratitude for the favour that has been done for him. Of course, we are unspeakably grateful for what Jesus has done for us, but it's not gratitude that controls Paul. Something else is going on here.

Paul explains in verses 14-15 why he is driven and controlled to live the way he does. He says 'We are controlled by the love of Christ because we have come to a conclusion; we have become convinced of a certain truth'.

He is convinced that one has died for all. So far, so good. But here's the twist: notice what Paul says next—because the logical conclusion of Paul is not the one we would draw.

Based on what we've studied so far in our seminar, we would say: one died for all so that all could escape death and live forever in God's kingdom. Jesus died for us, we might say, so that we could escape death.

But that's not what Paul says. He says: **one has died for all, therefore all have died**.

The logical result of Christ dying for all, says Paul, is that we all died.

It's not that Christ died so I would avoid death, so that I would never die. He died so that I **would** die. His death was my death. When he died, I died.

In other words, Christ died not only as a substitute but also as a **representative**. Not only **instead** of me, taking God's anger in my place; but also taking God's anger **as** me.

It's a bit like our politicians, who are our representatives. We elect them. They don't vote in the parliament or congress instead of us, as if it's them or us. They vote **for** us, as our local representatives. Their vote is really our vote.

So Christ didn't just die instead of us; he also died for us, as our representative. His death means that our death has also taken place. When he died, the death we rightly face as sinners took place. His death was our death—provided of course that he is our representative, and that we are in his electorate, his constituency, his electoral district.

Christ becomes our representative when we turn to him; when we enter his realm, his kingdom, and accept and acknowledge him as our Lord—or as the New Testament often puts it, when we put our faith in him, our reliance and dependent trust in him. When we cease trying to live as sinful autonomous rebels in all our independence and arrogance, and turn back to him as our rep, our head, our Lord, putting all our trust and faith and confidence in him—then we become one with him. It's as if Christ is the electoral district, and we leave our wretched home in the domain of darkness and go and live in him. This is how Paul describes it in verse 18. If anyone is "in Christ", he is a new creation.

Now if we are "in Christ", if he is our Lord and representative, then we receive the benefits of what he has done as if we ourselves had done it—so that when he died on the cross, it was also our death. And when he rises from the dead, then he rises for us as our representative as well. This is why Paul is confident that he will one day rise from the dead—because if he is one with Christ, and united with him, then Christ's death means our death, and Christ's resurrection means our resurrection.

This is why the love of Christ in dying for us as our substitute and representative controls Paul. Because if Christ has died, then Paul has died. His old life is over. It's gone. The rebel. The sinner. The old Paul, who lived for himself and his false gods. That life has ended. It received its just penalty on the cross with Jesus.

Now the purpose, says Paul, the very reason that Christ died as our representative, was so that our old rebellious life might die on the cross with him, and we would be liberated and raised up to live a new life—no longer rebellious, no longer obsessed with Self, but now living for him—the rightful Lord and ruler of all; the one we're united with, one with, submitting to, trusting in.

This is why Paul has no other option. This love of Christ by which he died and was raised constrains and compels and controls Paul. If he is going to join himself to Christ and thus receive the benefit of dying with Christ on the cross, then his old life is over. He is a completely new person; he has a new Spirit inside him. He is compelled to lead a completely new life—no longer for his own rebellious Self, which is now dead, but for Christ.

> ...and he died for all, that those who live might no longer live for themselves but for him who for their sake died and was raised. (2 Cor 5:15)

Do you see what this means for the course of our lives? It means that we actually have two lives to think about: the first is the one that we lived up until the time we were united with Christ—and that life is now over, crucified on the cross with Jesus. His death was our death.

The life we now live is a new creation, a completely new existence in which we no longer live for ourselves but for him who for our sake died and was raised.

5. Discussion and prayer

Give participants the opportunity for discussion, questions and comments on the input. Leave some time at the end for a few people to close in prayer.

Timing: 10-15 minutes

Seminar 7
Transformation

About this seminar

Building on the foundation of seminar 6, this seminar goes on to look at the nature of the new life we now live in Christ. We start by thinking about the ongoing presence of sin in the life of the believer. If we have died with Christ, and now live a new life in him, why do we still sin? Answer: it is because our new life in Christ is above; it is hidden, and we now live with 'a foot in two worlds'—as members of Christ's eternal kingdom, but also as people who still live in a sinful world, and with sin still dwelling in our personalities.

This leads us to see a fuller picture of God's agenda for us: it is not only to transfer us to the kingdom of his Son but also to transform us as well; to make us more like Jesus.

1. Discussion: Does it really matter how we live?

Have this discussion in the whole group. You might want to ask someone in advance to be the person whom everyone else is trying to persuade.

Timing: 20 minutes

Imagine a Christian friend said something like this to you: "I kind of know that I should try to be godly in my life as a Christian, but to be honest I'm not that motivated. I know that Jesus has paid for my sins, and that God has forgiven me. And I know that when I sin in the future—which I will!—he will forgive me then as well. So does it really matter all that much if my godliness doesn't improve?"

Choose one person in the group to 'be' this person. Try to persuade him or her that it really does matter how we live our lives as Christians.

After you've done this for a few minutes, write down together the most effective or useful arguments and Bible passages that came up in your 'debate'.

....

....

....

....

....

....

2. Input: The logic of the Christian life

Play video clip 9 here, or give your own talk based on its content.

Timing: 15 minutes

Script:

In our last two seminars we have seen that God's agenda, his plan, his purpose in this world, is to transfer forgiven rebels like us out of the domain of darkness and into the eternal kingdom of his Son; and that he does this by sending his Son to die as our substitute and representative.

If we are united with Christ by putting our faith and trust in him, then his death becomes our death. Our old life is finished, and we now live a new life to serve him.

But this raises a disturbing question: if we have died with Christ and have made such a radical break with our old life, if we now belong to his kingdom rather than to the domain of darkness, **then why do sinful thoughts and actions seem to be so stubbornly persistent in our lives?** And let's face it—they are! In fact, sometimes the longer you are Christian, the more aware you become of just how deeply sinfulness is rooted down in your personality.

What are we to make of this? What are we to do about it? How does the continuing presence of sin in our lives fit in with God's agenda for us?

Well, to answer this hugely important question, we are going to delve into Colossians—the letter that you've been reading in your one-to-one get-togethers.

We're going to spend some time in Colossians 3, because in this extraordinary passage Paul takes the ideas we looked at last time (about us being united with Christ in his death) and pushes them further, explaining exactly how they relate to the sin in our lives.

Let's read the first four verses:

> If then you have been raised with Christ, seek the things that are above, where Christ is, seated at the right hand of God. ² Set your minds on things that are above, not on things that are on earth. ³ For you have died, and your life is hidden with Christ in God. ⁴ When Christ who is your life appears, then you also will appear with him in glory. (Col 3:1-4)

Paul says here much of what he said in 2 Corinthians 5—that Christ's death is our death; that we have 'died' with him.

But in this passage he goes further and says that Christ's resurrection is also our resurrection. We **have been raised with Christ**, and our **life is hidden with Christ in God**.

The risen Jesus sits at God's right hand above, and that's where our true life now is. Because we're one with Christ, united with him, then we belong where he is, in his eternal kingdom. Our membership of that kingdom depends entirely on us being 'in him', part of him, united with him by faith, so that where he is, we are also.

But it's a hidden life. It is above. And it will only come into full view on that great day when Jesus comes again in all his glory. And then who we really are, what our life really is, will also be apparent to everyone.

But in the meantime, we live with 'a foot in two worlds'. We have been transferred out of the domain of darkness and into the kingdom of God's beloved Son. We really belong to Christ and the next world, because we have died and been raised up with him. But we also still live in this present evil age, and the sin of this age still dwells with us and in us.

For Paul, this presents not so much a problem as a challenge and an urgent task. Did you notice the two commands in those first four verses of Colossians 3?

> If then you have been raised with Christ, **seek the things that are above**, where Christ is, seated at the right hand of God. ² **Set your minds on things that are above**, not on things that are on earth. ³ For you have died, and your life is hidden with Christ in God. ⁴ When Christ who is your life appears, then you also will appear with him in glory. (Col 3:1-4)

If our old life has died, and our new life is hidden with Christ above, then that's where we should focus our eyes and our minds and our attention, says Paul. That's what we should earnestly seek and desire.

And if that is what we should set our minds and hearts on, what should be our attitude to the sin that is still in our lives? Paul has a simple recommendation: kill it. That's what he says next in the passage:

> **Put to death** therefore what is earthly in you: sexual immorality, impurity, passion, evil desire, and covetousness, which is idolatry. [6] On account of these the wrath of God is coming. [7] In these you too once walked, when you were living in them. [8] But now you must **put them all away**: anger, wrath, malice, slander, and obscene talk from your mouth. [9] Do not lie to one another, seeing that you have put off the old self with its practices [10] and have put on the new self, which is being renewed in knowledge after the image of its creator. (Col 3:5-10)

Notice what Paul doesn't say. He doesn't say: you should put to death all that is earthly in you, because that way you might manage to get into heaven! Quite the contrary: he says that because you are **already** in heaven in Christ, it's time to live that way and to get rid of all that remains of your old earthly life.

Notice also that he doesn't say: well, you're already raised above in Christ, so it probably doesn't matter all that much what you do here on earth. No! He says: because you are raised with Christ above, start living that way. Your old life, your old self, is dead and gone—so get rid of anything that belongs to that old life.

This is the fundamental logic of the Christian life: because of what Christ has done for us, and because we have died and been raised up with Christ, we now live a new life where we put sin to death and clothe ourselves with the character and attitudes and behaviours of the age to come, which is our real home.

This is what Paul goes on to say in the rest of this amazing chapter. The Christian life is not just killing sin and getting rid of it day by day; it's also putting on the clothes of the kingdom. It's dressing like we belong to Christ.

> **Put on then**, as God's chosen ones, holy and beloved, compassionate hearts, kindness, humility, meekness, and patience, [13] bearing with one another and, if one has a complaint against another, forgiving each other; as the Lord has forgiven you, so you also must forgive. [14] And above all these put on love, which binds everything together in perfect harmony. (Col 3:12-14)

So God's purpose in uniting us with Christ in his death and raising us up to a new life with him, hidden above, is not that we would stay the same, but that we would be transformed into the likeness of Christ; that we would be who we were created to be: men and women who live as the image of our creator.

God's plan is not just to **transfer** us from darkness to the kingdom of his Son, but also to **transform** us into the image of his Son.

And so perhaps we should expand our summary of God's agenda for the course of our lives.

God's agenda is to **transfer forgiven rebels** like us out of the domain of darkness and into his eternal kingdom, and to **transform us towards maturity** in Christ as we wait for his return.

Or we could add to that simple diagram:

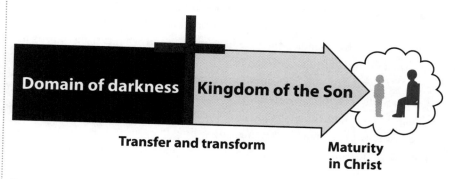

Because we have died in Christ and our life is now hidden with him in heaven, God's agenda for our lives is that we grow towards maturity in Christ as we wait for his return; that we leave the domain of darkness and get rid of all that remains of its influence in our lives.

Now, some of you might be thinking that this all sounds very well, but maybe a bit overly spiritual. When are we going to talk about the really big issues that I face in my life? About work and finances and relationships and marriage and family and all the rest?! About tiredness and stress and dissatisfaction? Isn't that what we're doing this course for—to talk about the big issues that run through the course of my life?

Well, that's the thing. On God's agenda, seeing us transferred and transformed **is** the big issue. This is where God's agenda collides with our own, and rewrites it.

You see, what is the one overriding thing that God really wants you to do for the rest of your life? What is to be your top priority? What is the dominating goal that he wants you to fix your eyes and mind and heart on?

It's not to have a good and fulfilling career.

It's not to build up financial security.

It's not to find the perfect man or woman to marry.

It's not to give your children the best in life.

It's not to have a healthy body or lifestyle.

It's not to enjoy all the good things of his creation.

And it's not even to go to church.

God's singular agenda item, under which everything else fits, is to transfer us into his kingdom and transform us step by step to be like Jesus Christ, whose death was our death and whose life is now our life. He wants us to fix our eyes and hearts and minds not on all the earthly things that crowd our agenda but on Christ above, where our true life is. And the consequence of this will be a consistent striving to put to death the sinfulness that belongs to this earthly life, and to clothe ourselves in the character of Jesus, the Lord of the age to come.

This is what truly matters to God. It matters far more to him than what career we have or how much money we have or what school our kids go to or where we go on holidays. And when we grasp that putting sin to death and clothing ourselves in the character of Christ is God's number one priority for us—the number one item on his agenda—then we have understood what it really means to be a Christian, and to live a Christian life.

Now you may still have questions about just how exactly you put sin to death in your life and clothe yourself with the character of Christ, and we'll come back to that shortly. But first, let's pause and consider where we've come to. We've started to see how God's agenda rewrites ours—how his priorities in the world should revolutionize our priorities in our lives. We might want to modify our summary statement like this:

> **Because God's agenda is**
> - **to transfer forgiven rebels into Christ's kingdom**
> - **and to transform us to be like Christ**
>
> **then our agenda is**
> - **to press forward towards maturity in Christ by putting sin to death and clothing ourselves in his character.**

Is that what your life is about?

3. Group discussion

Take some time to talk together about the video content. Throw the discussion open for questions and comments. To get things moving, you could use some discussion starter questions like these:

- How do you react to this vision of what God says our lives are about?
- Is this how you see your Christian life? Why/why not? What other priorities tend to dominate your life?
- Do you ever think about putting sin "to death" in your life? How would you go about this?

Timing: 10 minutes

4. Input: A killer's guide to sin

Play video clip 10 here, or give your own talk based on its content.

Timing: 7 minutes

Script:

We started this seminar by asking why sin is still in our lives if we have begun this radical new life in Christ.

As we have seen, the answer is that we should expect sin to continue to be with us as Christians. It is part of having a foot in two worlds—of continuing to live an earthly life with all its habitual sin, even though our real life really belongs to the next world in Christ.

So we should not be surprised when we find earthly sinful attitudes, thoughts and actions still present in our lives. The ongoing sin in our lives is like an enemy within our gates, a traitor who wants to sell us out to the opposition. We should not be surprised it is there, but neither should we be relaxed about it being there. And if we leave it unchecked, it will do us enormous harm. Paul's instruction is very clear: put to death whatever is earthly in you. Our attitude to sin should be cutthroat. We should aim to exterminate it, and to replace it with the godly, holy, loving character of Christ.

But how do we do this?

In Colossians, we are told of three weapons we can use in the fight to kill sin in our lives.

1. Our mind

The first weapon is our mind. Paul urges us to set our minds on things above, to make Christ above our mental focus, not earthly things. What do you fill your mind with? What do you read and watch and talk about? Do you make it a daily discipline to focus your thoughts and eyes and heart on where your life truly is, hidden with Christ above, waiting to be revealed? Or do the days and weeks go past without you pausing to direct your thoughts and attention to what is truly important, to the eternal kingdom you now belong to in Christ?

There are numerous ways to "set your minds on things that are above", and they are all versions of filling our minds with God's word. You can read and ponder a passage of Scripture. You can listen to a sermon on your iPod. You can read a good Christian book. You can simply mull over all that God has done for you in Christ. But the important thing is that you set your mind and heart and attention where it belongs: on Christ above.

2. Each other

The second weapon is related to the first. **The second weapon is each other.** God has given us each other to help us keep focused, to direct each other's attention to

Christ, to exhort and encourage each other, to speak the Word to each other. You see it in Colossians 3:16 where Paul urges them to "Let the word of Christ dwell in you richly, teaching and admonishing one another in all wisdom".

Other Christians speaking the word of truth to us—this is another invaluable weapon in the fight to kill off sin, whether in one-to-one meetings, in our families, in small groups, or in the large group at church.

3. Prayer

Both of these weapons depend on the third for true effectiveness. **The third weapon is prayer.** God graciously invites us to **ask him** to change us and to kill sin in our lives, and by the power of his Spirit he answers this prayer. We see Paul praying like this for the Colossians in chapter 1, starting at verse 9:

> And so, from the day we heard, we have not ceased to pray for you, asking that you may be filled with the knowledge of his will in all spiritual wisdom and understanding, [10] so as to walk in a manner worthy of the Lord, fully pleasing to him, bearing fruit in every good work and increasing in the knowledge of God. [11] May you be strengthened with all power, according to his glorious might, for all endurance and patience with joy...
> (Col 1:9-11)

This of course is another powerful way that we can help each other to make progress in putting off sin and putting on Christ: we can pray for each other, as Paul does here for the Colossians. It's a marvellous example and model for our prayers—the way he longs for them to grow and increase in the knowledge of God's will, to bear fruit, to please him, to walk in a manner worthy of him. Pray this for yourself, and pray it for others.

So the task is clear enough, and the weapons are close at hand. When are you going to start fighting?

5. Discussion and prayer

Divide into triplets, and talk about the sins in your life that you need to put to death. Pray for each other.

Timing: 15 minutes

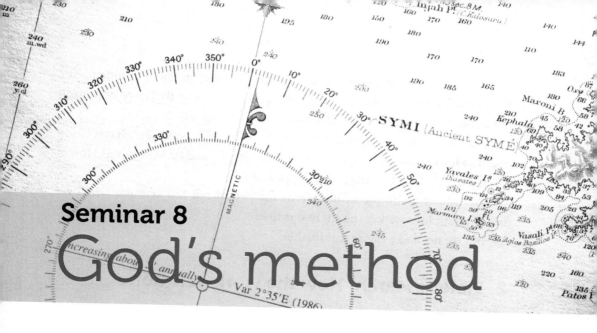

Seminar 8
God's method

About this seminar

In this seminar, we start to make the connection between striving towards Christlikeness ourselves (because of who we are in Christ), and helping others do the same.

We make this connection by thinking through how God advances his agenda in the world—that is, through the three P's of **p**roclamation, **p**rayer and **p**eople. The key point is that the **p**eople are not just paid ministers and pastors and evangelists, but all Christians. We all have a role in prayerfully speaking God's word to others to see them make progress towards maturity in Christ.

1. Introduction

Read through this introduction together.

Timing: 3 minutes

We've seen that God's agenda in our world and for our lives is to transfer forgiven rebels like us out of darkness into his eternal kingdom, and to transform us towards maturity in Christ as we wait for his return, and thus bring great glory to his Son.

We've also seen that this worldwide plan and agenda of God intersects with our own lives as we put our faith in Christ; as we are united with him in his death and raised up to a new life in him.

And in our last seminar, we saw that we take part in God's agenda in our lives by setting our minds and hearts on Christ above, and therefore by putting sin to death and clothing ourselves with the character of Christ.

But there is another question that we haven't really faced yet: what is God's **method** for pursuing this great work of transferring and transforming? How is he doing it? What's his strategy, his approach?

We caught a glimpse of it towards the end of our last seminar when we talked about how we kill the sin in our lives.

But we need to explore this further.

2. Bible research: How the work gets done

Do this exercise in the whole group.

Timing: 45 minutes

A. Read Colossians 1:3-8 and 4:2-6.

(i) What method does God use to transfer people into his kingdom?

(ii) Who does the work?

B. Read Colossians 1:9-10, 1:28-29, 2:6-8, 3:1-4 and 3:15-16.

(i) What means does God use for transforming people towards maturity in Christ?

(ii) Who does the work?

C. See if you can summarize what God's method is for pursuing his agenda in people's lives.

D. Now look up the following passages. What do they say about the role of every Christian in advancing God's agenda in the world?

- Matthew 28:16-20

- Romans 15:14-15

- 1 Corinthians 10:31-11:1

- 1 Corinthians 14:26

- 1 Corinthians 15:58, 16:10

- Philippians 1:3-7

- Philippians 1:27-30

- Philippians 4:14-19

- Hebrews 3:12-13

E. What conclusions would you draw from these passages?

F. How do you think the role of every Christian relates to the role of people with particular gifts or responsibilities (like pastors, teachers, and so on)?

G. How do you feel about your conclusions? Do any problems or obstacles spring to mind?

3. Input: God's strategy involves us

Play video clip 11 here, or give your own talk based on its content.

Timing: 18 minutes

Script:

There are many ways, I suppose, that you could summarize the method God is using to advance his work in our world—the **strategy** or **means** that he is using to transfer people into his kingdom and transform them to be like Christ. You could say that it is through his word and Spirit. Or that it is via the growth of the gospel, which is like a spreading plant that is bearing fruit all over the world.

One rather nice way to capture the ideas that have come out of the passages we've been studying is to say that God's method involves three P's.

1. Proclamation

The first is **proclamation**—that is, God's method involves words being spoken and taught and preached and pronounced and proclaimed, or whatever other speaking word you want to use. What happened in the lives of the Colossians is repeated all over the New Testament. They heard "the word of the truth", the gospel of God's grace, and they put their trust in it and it bore rich fruit in their lives. Their lives were turned completely around; so much so that Paul says they "died" and rose to a completely new life with Christ. And they heard the gospel because good old Epaphras came along and spoke some words to them.

And it was also by words that they were to grow and be transformed—by growing in knowledge and wisdom, and by letting the word of Christ dwell in them richly, such that Christ became the focus of their minds and hearts.

Now this word that is proclaimed and spoken and taught is the Word that we have recorded for us in the Bible. And God's method is to keep sowing the seed of this biblical word everywhere—whether in the lives of people who are not Christians so that they can be transferred into the kingdom, or in the lives of people who are already Christians so that they can grow and be transformed.

So the first P is **proclamation**.

2. Prayer

But there is an equally vital second P, and that is **prayer**. We can speak and teach and proclaim God's word as much as we like, but unless God brings real change in people's hearts as they listen, our speaking will be unfruitful. As Paul says in 1 Corinthians 3: "I planted, Apollos watered, but God gave the growth."

God accompanies our speaking and proclaiming of the Word with his own work—the work of his Spirit in people's hearts and lives. And this is why the second P is **prayer**. We need to express our faith and trust in God's work by **asking** and **begging** him to work in people's hearts, to graciously use the words we speak to transfer people from darkness to light—because changing a heart is something you and I could never do. We can speak a word, but we can't reach into people's chests and do surgery on their hearts to bring new life. Only God can do that.

And so all our **proclaiming** and speaking should be accompanied with **prayer**, asking God to do his part.

3. People

The third P seems a bit obvious, but it is really important. The third P is **people**. God uses people to do the proclaiming and the praying.

I guess, if he wanted to, God could just broadcast his word from the skies, or write it in the clouds; and if he wanted to, he could simply act in people's hearts whether we prayed for it or not. But amazingly, God chooses to work through weak and fallible human people to do his work in the world.

But which people?

The verses we have looked at in the New Testament make it very clear that it is people like us—very ordinary and sinful and inadequate people like you and me. Just as God uses the weak and foolish message of a man crucified on a cross to bring salvation to the world, so he uses jars of clay like us to proclaim it.

And it's not just specialists who do this, like paid ministers and pastors and evangelists. God uses all his people to speak the Word and to pray for its effectiveness. Of course, pastors and ministers and evangelists have a particular role in leading God's people in this task—in setting an example, in training, in having responsibilities for oversight, and so on—but it is the privilege and responsibility of every Christian to be part of God's cosmic agenda, his incredible work in the world—to be the means by which God pursues his agenda.

There is really only one kind of disciple of Jesus—the kind who has died with Jesus and been raised to a new life with Jesus, and who is charged by Jesus with the joyful (although sometimes scary) task of making other disciples: of speaking the Word to people and praying for them. We saw this in Colossians—how the Colossians in chapter 3 were to let the Word dwell among them richly. They were to admonish and speak to one another for each other's benefit. And then in chapter 4, we saw that they were all to speak to outsiders, to seek to bring a word to them that was gracious and helpful and salty.

Now this doesn't mean that we are all preachers, or that there is only one way of speaking the Word to another person. There is a multitude of ways, because we have a multitude of abilities and opportunities and circumstances.

We'll talk further about what these different opportunities might be, but let me just give two examples of what I mean.

- You're chatting after church with someone, and rather than just talking about how the week has been or what the kids are up to, you say something like, "You know, I really like the point the pastor made today when he said that our greatest need is for forgiveness. What did you think of it?"

  This is just a small word that might open up a conversation that dwells on the Word, and encourages another person. But it's a ministry that the pastor cannot have—he can't have that quiet friendly personal conversation with 150 people on a Sunday morning. It's a ministry that only you can have, because you are the one sitting next to that person and talking to them at that moment.

- Or take an everyday example: your workmate asks you what you did on the weekend, and you mention that you heard a really stimulating sermon in church, which said that the world's greatest problem is its need for forgiveness. And your workmate says, "Really? What about child poverty?" And you end up having a conversation about what forgiveness really is, why our physical needs and problems are not the only ones we have, and who knows what else.

You might not get far in your conversation, or it might lead somewhere. That's not up to you. God will do the work in people's hearts, not us. Our job is to speak the Word in whatever way we can, in whatever context we can, to any person we can (whether they're a Christian or not), praying that God would use our word (no matter how small it might be) to help that person make progress towards Christ, and towards maturity in Christ.

Because this is how it happens. God transfers and transforms people as his word is prayerfully spoken by one person to another.

This is a very concrete way in which God's agenda shapes our agenda. If we ourselves are God's chosen means for transferring and transforming people, then maybe we need to extend our summary of God's agenda for our lives.

You remember that in our last session we talked about an overriding priority and purpose in the course of our lives:

Because God's agenda is
- **to transfer us into Christ's kingdom**
- **and to transform us to be like Christ**

then our agenda is
- **to press forward towards maturity in Christ by prayerfully setting our hearts and minds on Christ in his word.**

We need to add to it. Our agenda is also:

- **to move others towards maturity in Christ by prayerfully speaking God's word to them.**

Now, there's more to say about all this—lots more—but before we pause to talk and pray together about all this, I want to sum up what we've been looking at in this seminar in a slightly different way.

So far, we've been talking about our lives and what they're about by talking about God's agenda—his priority list, as it were—and what that means for the agenda of our own lives. And we've arrived at the point where God's priorities to see people transferred and transformed have come to shape our priorities—for ourselves to grow like Christ, and for us to help others be transferred and transformed as well.

But another way of saying this is that God wants our hearts to be like his. He wants each of us to have a shepherd's heart.

God is the great shepherd. He loves and leads his sheep. And he sends us his Son to be the Good Shepherd who lays down his life for the sheep (as John 10 tells us).

If we are to become like Jesus, and to clothe ourselves in his character, then we need to develop the heart of a shepherd—a heart that longs to care for others, to feed and protect others, to love others, to see others grow and make progress, to lay down our lives for others—just like Jesus did.

Think about your neighbours, your workmates, your housemates, your spouse, your children, your family members, the people sitting next to you in church, the newcomers who walk in the church door. What does each one of them need? How can you help them? What could you do that would lead each one of them forward a little more towards Christ and godly maturity in him?

To be Christian is to have the heart of a shepherd who wants to lead others forward—in whatever way we can, large or small—so that they may come to know the Good Shepherd, and find life and salvation and freedom and maturity in him.

4. Discussion and prayer

Take some time to talk together about the video content. Throw the discussion open for questions and comments. As you do so, you might mention to people that during the intensive (which is coming up), you'll have more time to think all this through and to work out what it means for everyone.

To get things moving, you could use some discussion starter questions like these:

- What do you think of the three P's as a summary of God's method?
- How do you feel about being part of God's method for his work in the world? Humbled? Scared? Privileged?
- What obstacles and problems come to mind as you think about your own role in speaking God's word to others?

Then spend some time praying together.

Timing: 20 minutes

Intensive

About the intensive

The intensive consists of six parts/sessions, each of around 80-90 minutes. You could run it on two separate weekends (e.g. two consecutive Saturdays from 9:30 am to 3:30 pm). But it is better to run it on two days away together (e.g. all day Friday and Saturday; or starting with Friday evening and running through to Sunday lunchtime). There are huge benefits in being away together for an extended period of time—in building relationships within the group, but most importantly in giving people time to think and talk and pray away from the busyness of daily life.

The program for a two-day intensive would be something like this:

Day 1

Morning	Parts 1 and 2
Afternoon	Free time plus part 3
Evening	Social time or catch up on anything not yet finished in parts 1-3

Day 2

Morning	Parts 4 and 5
Afternoon	Free time plus part 6
Evening	Dinner together and then home

Part 1: Where we're up to

About this session

This first session aims to consolidate the big ideas of the course in the participants' minds; to pull together and summarize all that has been covered, and provide an opportunity for questions and discussion.

1. The story so far

Break into ad hoc subgroups (say, around four people per group), and get each group to do the revision exercise.

Timing: 30 minutes

See if you can complete the following summary of the course so far—from memory. If not, have a quick look back at each seminar in your workbook.

Seminar 2: God's creative purposes

A. What were God's purposes for humanity in creation?

B. We are God's creatures, created by him for particular reasons. What then should be our basic attitude or response towards God?

C. What does all this mean for the plans and agenda we have for our lives?

Seminar 3: What went wrong?

A. What was the essence of humanity's rebellion against God?

B. What was God's judgement against us?

C. Ecclesiastes spells out the realities of a world under God's judgement. What are the particular implications for the plans and dreams we have for our life here on earth?

Seminar 4: God's answer

A. God has an answer to the absurdity, injustice and evil of our judged world. In what three ways is this answer revealed?

B. What does 'the sufficiency of Scripture' mean?

C. What are the implications of the sufficiency of Scripture for understanding the agenda of our lives?

Seminar 5: God's agenda

A. What is God's ultimate plan or agenda for the world? How would you summarize it?

B. How does God's agenda address the basic problem of our world and our lives?

Seminar 6: Christ's death, my life

A. What does Paul mean in 2 Corinthians 5:14-15 when he says, "one has died for all, therefore all have died"?

B. How does this motivate us in our daily lives?

Seminar 7: Transformation

A. If our old self has died in Christ, why does sin still persist in our lives?

B. What is the basic motivation for seeking to kill sin in our lives, and to clothe ourselves in Christlike character?

C. How would you summarize God's agenda for our lives?

Seminar 8: God's method

A. What are the three P's by which God pursues his agenda in the world?

B. What is the role of every Christian in God's work in the world?

C. See if you can complete the summary of God's agenda that we came up with in seminar 8:

Because God's agenda is

- **to** _____ **us into** _____

- **and to** _____ **us to be** _____

then our agenda is

- **to** _____ **towards** _____ **by prayerfully**

  _____

- **and to move** _____ **towards** _____ **by prayerfully**

  _____.

Unanswered questions

Do you have any major unanswered questions arising out of the course so far?

- Things we've covered that you don't understand or aren't sure about

- Things we haven't covered yet

2. Group feedback

Gather back together and work through the eight seminar topics. Ask one group to contribute their summary for seminar 2; then ask a different group to contribute their summary for seminar 3; and so on. Have others add to each summary if they had something extra. The idea is to get everything solid in people's minds.

Then spend some time discussing the questions people raised. As a group, try to deal with as many of these as possible.

Timing: 30-40 minutes

Part 2: The disciple's commission

About this session

This session builds on seminar 8—about the role that we all have as disciples in seeking to move others forward in Christ. It does this in two ways:

- it digs down a little deeper biblically and theologically into the basis of our involvement in God's work in the world by looking at Jesus' commissioning of his disciples in Matthew 28
- it examines more practically what our involvement really means—in particular, by presenting a model of how to think about people and move them forward towards Christ and maturity in him.

1. Bible study: Matthew 28:16-20

You can do this Bible study in the whole group if you wish, or divide into smaller subgroups.

Timing: 20 minutes

Read Matthew 28:16-20.

A. What has the resurrected Jesus been given?

B. What does he tell his disciples to do, and in what time frame?

C. What do you think is the connection between your answers to A and B?

D. Is there anything in the passage to suggest that Jesus' command:

- only applies to the eleven disciples who first heard it?

- might apply to all his disciples?

2. Input: The disciple's commission

Play video clip 13 here, or give your own talk based on its content.

Timing: 18 minutes

Script:

In 1792, a young man named William Carey published a booklet entitled *An Enquiry into the Obligations of Christians to use Means for the Conversion of the Heathen*. In it, Carey argued against the dominant view of that time: that the Great Commission of Matthew 28—the passage you have just been studying—had been fulfilled by the first disciples and was not applicable to the church in succeeding generations. For Carey, this was simply ducking our responsibility. He saw the Great Commission as a duty and privilege for all generations—and thus began the modern missionary movement.

The point that Carey argued for so strongly is no longer controversial. Of course we should be sending out missionaries to the ends of the earth and seeking to reach the whole world for Christ. But is that really what Matthew 28 is primarily about? These momentous verses are worth a closer look, especially because they summarize a great deal of what we have already seen in this course.

When Jesus tells his astonished but also doubting disciples that, "All authority in heaven and on earth has been given to me", it shouldn't come as a surprise to them. For the previous three years, they had seen Jesus' authority every day—as he healed the sick, raised the dead, taught with authority, and even forgave sins. They had heard him say things like this:

> "When the Son of Man comes in his glory, and all the angels with him, then he will sit on his glorious throne. [32] Before him will be gathered all the nations, and he will separate people one from another as a shepherd separates the sheep from the goats." (Matt 25:31-32)

And now, in Matthew 28, they are standing in the presence of this Son of Man on a hillside in Galilee—the Man before whom all peoples, from every nation and tongue, will bow.

It is on this basis—the unique, supreme and worldwide authority of the risen Son of Man—that Jesus commissions his disciples to spread the word of his authority and lordship to everyone. As they go on their way, they are to make disciples of all nations, baptizing and teaching them to obey Jesus.

Whatever else baptism symbolizes or involves, here it refers to the initiation of disciples into repentance and submission to the authoritative Jesus, the reigning Lord of the world.

The "teaching" that the disciples are to do reproduces what Jesus himself has done with them. He has been their teacher throughout Matthew's Gospel and, as Jesus has taught them, they have grown in knowledge and understanding. The disciples are now, in turn, to not only initiate new disciples to be under the lordship of the worldwide King, but also teach them to obey everything commanded by their Master.

The making of disciples is not an instant process. It doesn't just involve conversion or initiation into Christ; it also involves growth and maturity, as the disciples learn to obey everything that Jesus has commanded. We often associate disciplemaking with evangelism and conversion, but it is much more comprehensive than that. It involves everything from our initial conversations with a non-Christian friend right through to our encouragement of someone who has been a Christian for 50 years. Because to make a disciple is teach someone to obey Jesus in everything—and that's a lifelong process!

The disciple-making commission that Jesus gives the disciples has no boundaries. It is universal. Because Jesus as **all** authority, his disciples are to make disciples of **all** nations. The authority of Jesus is not limited by anything. He is the Lord and Master of my street, my neighbours, my suburb, my workmates, my family, my city, my nation—and yes, the whole world. We would not ever want to stop sending missionaries to preach the gospel in far-flung places where it has not yet been heard, but we must also see disciple-making as the central task in our homes and neighbourhoods and churches—because the message of Jesus' universal authority needs to be heard there as well.

And Jesus' command is not only universal in its scope; it's also universal in its application. It is a command not just for the first eleven disciples but also for every disciple—if only because the time scale involved requires it. Jesus promises that he will be with his disciples always as they make disciples, "to the end of the age". The work of disciple-making is the central and abiding task of Jesus' disciples from the time of his resurrection and ascension until the time he returns at the end of the age. So far, it has been going on for 2000 years—which would be very difficult if the job was only for the eleven disciples who were there to hear the command when it was originally given.

Furthermore, the very nature of the task means that it generates not only new disciples, but also new disciple-makers. New disciples are to be taught to obey everything that the Lord Jesus Christ commanded. And it is hard to imagine a more significant or important command of Jesus than this one—his parting charge to make disciples of all nations. And so new disciples fall under exactly the same obligation as the original eleven disciples—they too are to obey Jesus' command to get on with the job of making disciples, of announcing the gospel of his lordship to all nations, and of seeing people grow to maturity as servants of the Lord Jesus Christ.

To be a disciple is to be a maker of disciples. And this fits very closely with what we have already seen is God's agenda for our lives. God's great plan is to glorify his Son Jesus as the Lord of the world, and to see people become his obedient disciples. Remember, in our last seminar, we summarized God's agenda like this:

Because God's agenda for the world is
- **to transfer forgiven rebels like us into Christ's kingdom**
- **and to transform us to be like Christ**

then his agenda for our lives is
- **for us to press forward towards maturity in Christ by prayerfully setting our minds on Christ in his word**
- **and for us to move others towards maturity in Christ by prayerfully speaking God's word to them.**

Or in terms of Matthew 28, our central and abiding concern is not only to learn to obey all that our Master Jesus has commanded, but also to make disciples who do the same: who submit to Christ as the Lord of all, and yearn to obey all his words.

Matthew 28 also helps us to see that our work of moving people towards maturity in Christ (or the making of disciples) is not a one-off or instantaneous process. It is a slow step-by-step process. We could add to the diagram we've been using to illustrate this.

At one level, there are only two kinds of people in the world: those still stuck in the domain of darkness and those who have been transferred into the kingdom of the Son.

But within those two broad categories there are common stages or phases that people go through.

Some are **far away**, with absolutely no knowledge of Jesus or contact with Christians.

Some have made **contact** with a Christian person, or know something vaguely about Christ.

Others have started **talking**, perhaps about spiritual or moral issues. They have begun to ask questions and to have genuine conversations.

Some have got to the point where someone else has actually told them the **gospel**—and with God's work in their heart, they have responded and turned to Christ for the forgiveness of their sins, and have been transferred from darkness to light and into the kingdom of the Son.

These are **new Christians** who need support and help and teaching to establish them securely and firmly in the faith.

Then comes the process of **growth** and maturation that continues throughout our Christian lives; a process that involves frequent **struggles** and setbacks. It also involves **training**—that is, being equipped to move others forward towards Christ: to go back and make contact with those who are far away; to talk to them and share the gospel with them; to follow them up as new Christians; and to encourage them for their growth.

You see, it's daunting to say that your charge and commission from Jesus himself is to be a maker of disciples! But if we break that down and say that your task is simply to shepherd the people you know just one step to the right, one step towards maturity in Christ—wherever they may be—well, that is more manageable. That is something I can do; it's something we can all do.

For someone who is far away, you might start by simply making contact with them and being friendly. For someone who you've started talking with about serious issues, you might start actually sharing the gospel with them. For someone who is a new Christian, you might work through some basic part of Christ's teaching. For someone who has been a Christian much longer, your role might be to help them persevere and grow in godliness amid life's troubles; or it might be to train them to be a disciple-maker (someone who goes back down the spectrum and helps others to make progress step by step).

There are countless ways we can shepherd people towards maturity in Christ—according to our opportunities, our circumstances and our own gifts and abilities. Let's pause and think about some of those ways.

3. Step by step

The goal here is to get people to start thinking through what the general principle means in daily practice. Start by reading through the examples below together. Then discuss/brainstorm your own ideas of how to move people forward step by step.

Beware the tendency to get away from Word ministry. Remember, we move people towards maturity in Christ by prayerfully sharing the Word with them in some way—whether by writing a note, or reading the Bible with them, or taking them to hear a sermon, or whatever. Keep focusing on this as you brainstorm.

Timing: 25-30 minutes

There are so many ways that we can move people step by step towards maturity in Christ, no matter where they are on the spectrum. Here are some examples:

- Sarah's teenage son is having real problems at school, and as they talk about it at night, she reassures him that God is stronger and more faithful than any friend, and prays with him.
- Bill is chatting to George after church, and shares with him how encouraged he was by a particular verse in the Bible that day.
- Michael meets every fortnight over breakfast with his mate Steve, who is a newish Christian. They use the *Just for Starters* studies to work through some of the basic issues of the Christian life.
- Warren goes to a Bible study group each week at Jim's house with six other people. He makes sure that he has read and thought about the passage before he goes, and prays that God would help him to say true and encouraging things in the group.
- Irene is quite elderly and finds it hard to get out, but she phones her

friend Jean every second day, talks to her about the Bible passage she has read that morning, and prays with her over the phone.

- Clare has been praying for her friend Shirley for months, and finally invites her to an evangelistic evening that her church is running. On the way home in the car, Clare talks to Shirley about the message, and does her best to answer Shirley's questions.
- Trevor rearranges his work schedule so that he can take each Wednesday morning off to teach Scripture classes in his local primary school. He and his wife end up doing this for many years, having an enormous impact on the lives of kids and teachers at their local school.
- At Phil's church, they take a few minutes each week during the Sunday meeting for a congregation member to give a testimony or to bring an encouraging word to the congregation. This Sunday it's Phil's turn, and he explains how the teaching of Ephesians 5 has turned his marriage around.[5]

Try coming up with some ideas of your own. Think of someone you know (Christian or non-Christian). What could you do to move them a step or two closer to Christ, and to maturity in Christ?

There are a number of ways you could do this. One suggestion: Ask someone in the group to name someone they know—a friend, a family member, a work colleague—anyone. Get the person to indicate where this person is on the spectrum (from **far away** to **growth** in Christ). Ask the group to brainstorm ways to move that person forward a step or two.

5   Taken from Colin Marshall and Tony Payne, *The Trellis and the Vine*, Matthias Media, Sydney, 2009, pp. 54-55.

Part 3: God's agenda and our work

About this session

Work is one of the massive issues we need to think through as we come to terms with God's agenda for our lives. Most of us have grown up with the idea that our work is what defines us, and many Christians simply adopt the standard worldly view of work without thinking too much about it. Some do it unconsciously—they simply partition off work from their Christian lives, and pursue a career like everyone else. God is something they 'do' in the time that is left over after work and on the weekends. Others pursue career success, and say that God is calling them to it and that their success and excellence brings honour to him.

In this session and the one following, we take a look at this issue and talk through the implications. The key idea to communicate is that God's agenda for our lives is not something separate or sealed off from our work (or from any aspect of our lives). God is not a ball to be juggled along with our work and our family and everything else. God's plan for us in Christ sets the agenda for every aspect of our lives. It permeates everything; it overlays everything.

In this session, we'll look at the Bible's teaching about work, and at how God's agenda shapes our attitude to work.

In the next session (part 4), we'll take some time to think and talk together about what this means for us, and to pray.

1. Input: What about work?

This opening video segment sets the scene for our examination of 'work' as one of the theatres or contexts in which we live out God's agenda for our lives. As usual, play the video (clip 14), or give your own presentation based on the script below.

Timing: 10 minutes

Script:

Let's remind ourselves of our summary of God's agenda for the world and our lives:

> **Because God's agenda for the world is**
> - **to transfer forgiven rebels like us into Christ's kingdom**
> - **and to transform us to be like Christ**
>
> **then his agenda for our lives is**
> - **for us to press forward towards maturity in Christ by prayerfully setting our minds on Christ in his word**
> - **and for us to move others towards maturity in Christ by prayerfully speaking God's word to them.**

But how does this extraordinary and challenging agenda relate to our daily work? We still have to go to work, or look after the kids, or go to university, or whatever it is we do. Should we just stop doing all these things and pursue God's agenda instead? If we **do** have to work, does God's agenda mean that our work is unimportant? Does it mean that God isn't interested in what we do between 9 and 5 (or, as it increasingly is, 8 and 6)?

And what of family life? For those in the family stage, life is very full and very busy—how does God's agenda fit into that? Is it something else I am supposed to squeeze in somehow?

Over the next couple of sessions we'll look at these issues and try to sort out how God's life-changing agenda intersects with the course of our daily lives.

Let's start with 'work'.

And let's start by asking: **what is 'work'?** We immediately tend to define 'work' in terms of a paid job of some kind, because that's what work means for a large proportion of people in the Western world. But of course in many parts of the world today, and in the time of the Bible, work was not necessarily done for wages—it was whatever people did to sustain their lives, whether in growing or gathering their food, or in providing clothes and shelter. Work is what the labourer does in the field; it is also what the exemplary woman of Proverbs 31 does in clothing her family and trading as a merchant. Work can be done in the home, or in the field, or in the marketplace. It can be done by men and women, by old and young.

Work is that activity whereby we apply thought and effort to what God has given us in creation so as to sustain and nourish our lives. This was the task given to Adam, the very first worker. In Genesis 2, we read that God had planted a garden in Eden, in the east, and caused every tree that is pleasant to the sight and good for food for to grow there.

Genesis 2:15 says that "The LORD God took the man and put him in the garden of Eden to work it and keep it". And in verses 18 and following, God makes the woman as a fit helper to the man in this task.

Work is part of God's good creative purposes. Humanity was to gain their food by working the garden and keeping it—that is, to do that which was necessary not only to derive food and sustenance from the earth, but also to shepherd and preserve those resources so that they would continue to provide food into the future.

And the garden is portrayed as a rich and abundant and enjoyable place to work and to eat.

However, there was one tree that was not to be the object either of work or of eating, and that was the tree of the knowledge of good and evil.

Genesis 3 tells the tragic story of humanity's decision to reach out and grab the fruit of that tree in rebellion against God. It's the story of mankind's rejection of God's rule, and of the resulting judgement that God decrees upon them.

And it has very significant implications for our understanding of work—for God's judgement is not only that Adam and Eve will be ejected from the beauty and abundance of the garden in Eden, but also that the ground will now be cursed. This is particularly directed to Adam, the one who was primarily given the task of working the garden:

> And to Adam he said, "Because you have listened to the voice of your wife and have eaten of the tree of which I commanded you, 'You shall not eat of it', cursed is the ground because of you; in pain you shall eat of it all the days of your life; [18] thorns and thistles it shall bring forth for you; and you shall eat the plants of the field. [19] By the sweat of your face you shall eat bread, till you return to the ground, for out of it you were taken; for you are dust, and to dust you shall return." (Gen 3:17-19)

Man's work is now marred by pain and struggle, and thwarted by thorns and thistles. And at the end of a life of painful toil, all he has to look forward to is death, and to returning to the dust from which he was taken.

This is the world in which mankind has worked ever since. It's the world in which the rest of the Bible unfolds, with all that it has to say about work.

Let's do some digging into the Bible now to see what it says.

2. Bible survey: The good and bad of work

Divide into subgroups and allocate the passages in the following table among the groups. Give them 30 minutes to cover as many passages as they can.

Then come back together and build up a composite picture of the Bible's teaching on work by answering the general questions (B and C below) in light of what each group has discovered. Allow 20 minutes for this general discussion.

Total timing: 30 + 20 = 50 minutes

A. Divide up the following Bible passages among your groups, and fill in the table. Not every passage will have something to say under each heading.

Passage	Good things about work	Not-so-good things about work	Good attitudes or approaches to work	Poor attitudes or approaches to work
Gen 11:1-9				
Eccl 2:1-11				
Eccl 2:18-26				
Eccl 4:4-8				
Eccl 5:18-20				
Eccl 9:9-10				
Prov 12:14				

Prov 18:9				
Prov 21:25				
Prov 23:4				
Prov 24:27				
Luke 12:13-31				
Eph 4:28				
2 Thess 3:6-12				
Col 3:22-24				
Jas 4:13-16				

B. Come back together as one whole group and pool your findings.

(i) What's good about work?

(ii) What's hard or difficult about work?

(iii) What wise or good attitudes or approaches to work did you find?

(iv) What harmful, wrong or foolish attitudes or approaches to work did you discover?

C. How does the Bible's teaching fit with your own experience of work?

(i) What do you enjoy about work?

(ii) What do you find difficult?

(iii) What good approaches to work have you observed or practised?

(iv) What poor or wrong attitudes have you observed or fallen into?

3. Input: Our work and God's agenda

Play video clip 15 here, or give your own talk based on its content. This input concludes part 3. We'll take up the issues and talk and pray about them in part 4 of the intensive.

Timing: 12 minutes

Script:

Given all that we have seen in the Bible, the love-hate relationship that most of us have with work should not come as a surprise.

Work is a basic and good part of God's world. It is the God-given way for us to survive and thrive in his creation—to get our food, to build our homes, to nourish and raise our children. And we often glimpse this goodness in the cleverness and productivity of human work, in the satisfaction we feel in a job well done, in the enjoyment of savouring the fruits of our labours—and most particularly in the 'lostness' and dislocation we feel if we cannot find a job.

We love work, in the sense that we can't and don't want to do without it. But we also hate work, because all human work takes place in the shadow of God's judgement. Despite all the incredible gains in technology, the basic nature of work has not changed. It is still a source of frustration, anger, boredom, dissatisfaction and pain.

It is like so many other good things in God's creation. We can see its goodness and worth; and yet we can also see its frustrations, errors, injustices and evils.

In fact, work itself can become an evil if it is the instrument by which we assert our independence of God, and our desire to secure a future without him. This is the basic message of the tower of Babel in Genesis 11. It is also the sobering story in Luke 12 of the rich fool who trusts so implicitly in the value of his labours and his success that he forgets (or perhaps more accurately, ignores) the God who holds his life in his hand. This too is the stark and realistic message of Ecclesiastes. The injustice and unpredictability of the world can make our grand work projects fail or look foolish; at other times we may succeed in our work, but only for the benefit of someone else, not ourselves. And the grim inevitability of death mocks all our attempts to control our future through our own labours.

So how does work, with its joys and frustrations, fit into God's agenda for our lives?

Christians make two mistakes in seeking to live as Christians and as workers.

The first is the error of Babel and of the rich fool: it is to invest our work with too much significance, as if what we do to earn our bread is what matters most about us—that we are a doctor, or a lawyer, or a teacher, or a nurse, or a successful businessman. This is really the mistake of crafting our own agenda in life—to have a successful career; to **be** someone; to achieve great things—rather than letting the God who made us and who redeemed us in Christ write the agenda of our lives, and set our priorities.

And of all the agenda items that people often put at the top of their list—and thus displace God with—work is one of the most common. Our modern Western culture places enormous emphasis on what we do. Our job defines us. It tells the world whether we are important or not, interesting or not, worth paying attention to or not. Why else is the first question we ask at a party always, "And what do you do?" Why else is working in the home not really classed as work or as a 'job'? It is because it doesn't confer status or achievement, nor is it rewarded with a fat pay packet.

When God calls on us to screw up the piece of paper on which our life's agenda is written, and accept from him a new agenda—which is really a description of what it means to become a Christian—career success is the agenda item that many of us find hardest to part with. Don't get me wrong: God may bless you with career success; he may give you great joy and satisfaction in your work. And if he does, thank him for it and don't be arrogant in that success. But don't **run after** career success. Don't long for it and seek it. Don't fix your eyes and heart on it, because where your heart is there your agenda will be also.

Now that we are a new creation in Christ, living a completely new life in him, we are to fix our eyes and heart on him, and consequently on putting sin to death in our lives and clothing ourselves with Christ's character. And, in love, we are to do all we can to shepherd others forward as well, to become more like Jesus.

If this is our overriding agenda in life, then it helps us to avoid the second common mistake we make when it comes to work, which is to think that God's new agenda in our lives has nothing to do with our work—as if work is a fairly meaningless and inconsequential thing we just have to do, so that when we've finished it each week, we can get on with God's agenda in our lives.

On the contrary: work is one of the many spheres of our lives **in which we work out God's agenda day by day**; it is one area where we seek to move forwards to maturity in Christ, and to help others do so as well.

What does that mean?

Well, for one thing, it means that as we work, we look for whatever opportunities we can to put sin to death in our lives and to clothe ourselves in Christ's character. This might mean striving to display honesty in our work, trustworthiness, diligence, forgiveness, grace, patience, kindness, and the rest of the fruit of the Spirit as well, including self-control—especially self-control!

But it also means relating and interacting with people at work in such a way as to help them take a step towards Christ. If all Christians are not only disciples but also makers and growers of other disciples, then work is an ideal place to live this out. It's where most of us spend most of every day!

I often think of Paul's words to the Colossians when I think of being a disciple-maker at work:

> Walk in wisdom toward outsiders, making the best use of the time. [6] Let your speech always be gracious, seasoned with salt, so that you may know how you ought to answer each person. (Col 4:5-6)

Impeccable and impressive behaviour, coupled with gracious, salty, interesting, gospel-directed speech. There's an ideal to aspire to!

What we have seen in this session about work really fits into the big picture that we've been sketching and filling in during the entire course.

We live in a world created good by God, that still reveals joy and beauty, but which is also rebellious against God and judged by him. We experience this in our work, and for that matter in all the other spheres of life—in our friendships, in our marriages, in our families, in our plans, in everything. Flashes of goodness, beauty, satisfaction and joy in all these areas remind us that God did make this world good. But we cannot escape the evil, the sin, the frustration, the injustice, the judgement. It renders futile and absurd our grand attempts to master this world, or to create a future for ourselves through our work or our family.

Our future is in Christ—because we have died with him, and been born anew to a new life that is hidden with him in heaven. And we await the day when he comes and is revealed and our new life is revealed with him.

In the meantime, we seek that which is above, not that which is here on earth. And we put off the old earthly ways, and put on the character of the new kingdom.

We still have to live in this world; and we will still experience all its joys as well as its sorrows and evils. But it doesn't set our agenda. Our agenda is set by the world to come, by the plans God has for us in Christ in his kingdom. **That's** what we seek and focus on and set our hearts and minds on in all areas of our life—including in our work.

Part 4: Talk and pray

About this session

This session has three goals, and you may well find that you don't get through everything. You may want to extend the session, or continue it after a break. Play it by ear. The three goals are:

- To take time to talk and pray about the personal implications of what we looked at in part 3 about work.
- To see how the Bible's teaching about work represents a pattern that can be applied to many other areas of our lives.
- To talk and pray about another aspect of our lives (e.g. family) using the same pattern of thinking.

1. Let's talk

This discussion needs to take place in a sufficiently small group for people to feel comfortable to talk openly and honestly—say, in groups of five or six at most. So divide up according to how many people you have doing the course.

In this discussion about work, we are setting up a pattern that we will apply in the second half of the session to other aspects of our lives. Depending on the composition of the group, you may wish to shorten the work discussion and spend more time on the second half of the session (below).

Timing: 40 minutes

In our last session, we covered lots of ground and raised plenty of meaty issues. Now we're going to take some time to talk through our questions, and to pray.

A. We talked about two common mistakes Christians make in thinking about their work. The first is the mistake of Babel and of the rich fool: to invest our work, and the fruits of our work, with too much significance; to make 'a successful career' the main agenda item of our life.

(i) How does this attitude tend to show itself, do you think—in our day-to-day lives as well as in the bigger decisions we make?

(ii) Where do you see this tendency in yourself (if at all)?

(iii) What can you do about it?

B. The other common problem is to seal our work life off from God, as if it doesn't matter to him what we do between 9 and 5 each day.

(i) How would this attitude show itself?

(ii) Where do you see this tendency in yourself (if at all)?

(iii) What can you do about it?

C. A Christian friend says to you: "I want to glorify God in my work, which means I'm going to strive for excellence and success in my field. I want to honour him by being the best I can be." How would you respond?

D. Spend some time talking about how you think God wants us to pursue his agenda in our lives as we go to work each day, based on what we have looked at in the course so far.

(i) In what ways could you press forward towards maturity in Christ in the way you work? What sins do you need to put to death? What Christlike character do you need to put on?

(ii) How could you move others towards maturity in Christ at your work? Who do you relate to often at work? How could you move them one step forwards?

E. Pray together about the challenges of your work lives. Share the particular struggles you have, and ask God to help you live out his agenda at work.

2. Taking it further

This discussion takes the general principles we discovered when we looked at the area of work, and applies them to other areas of our lives.

Timing: 30-40 minutes

Boiling it all down, we could summarize our discussion of work like this:

A. **Work** is a good creation of God for our benefit and growth. And even though **work** is marred by sin and the Fall, we still find joy and satisfaction in it, and should receive it as God's good gift with thanksgiving.

B. It is possible to misuse this gift by using our devotion to **work** to assert our independence from God; by making success and satisfaction in our **work** the real goal and agenda of our lives; by partitioning our **work** off from God and his agenda for our lives.

C. But God's agenda is for every aspect of our lives. It overlays and permeates everything we do. So God wants us to view our **work** as one of the areas in life in which we pursue his agenda, not ours—by pursuing Christlikeness in all that we do at **work**, and by seeking to move others in our **workplace** towards Christ as we relate to them.

D. This agenda influences not only how we behave in our **workplace**, but also the decisions we make about **work**—how much time we devote to it, how ambitiously we pursue it, and what we're prepared to give up in order to gain success.

This basic pattern of biblical thinking can be applied to nearly every other important area of our lives. For example, read back through the four points above, and replace the words 'work' and 'workplace' with the word 'family'.

You can try the same exercise with 'sport' or 'music' or 'education' (making adjustments here and there). All of these good gifts of God can also end up being a means of actually rebelling against God and writing our own agenda in life.

Choose one of these areas that is particularly relevant to you as a group, and work through the following questions.

A. It's possible to invest _____ with too much significance; to make success and happiness in _____ the main agenda item of our life.

(i) How does this attitude tend to show itself, do you think—in our day-to-day lives as well as in the bigger decisions we make?

(ii) Where do you see this tendency in yourself (if at all)?

(iii) What can you do about it?

B. The other common problem is to seal our _____ life off from God, as if it doesn't matter to him how we behave or how we relate to people when we are _____.

(i) How would this attitude show itself?

(ii) Where do you see this tendency in yourself (if at all)?

(iii) What can you do about it?

C. Spend some time talking about how you think God wants us to pursue his agenda in our lives through _____, based on what we have looked at in the course so far.

(i) In what ways could you press forward towards maturity in Christ in this area? What sins do you need to put to death? What Christlike character do you need to put on?

(ii) How could you move others towards maturity in Christ in your _____? Who could you move one step forwards? What's the next thing you could do for or with them?

D. Pray together about the challenges of your _____ lives. Share the particular struggles you have, and ask God to help you live out his agenda in this area.

Part 5: We're in this together

About this session

Having laid so much groundwork about what God is doing in our world and how that relates to our lives, thinking about church and how that fits in is relatively straightforward. In one sense, church is where we pursue God's agenda together; in another sense, church is the outcome of God's agenda—a people of his own gathered around Christ for eternity.

1. Introduction

So far in *The Course of Your Life*, we've talked a lot about God and his plan or agenda for our lives. But we've done this mostly at an individual level, thinking about the course of our own particular lives.

But of course, we're not isolated individuals. We are each part of a network of families and neighbourhoods and friends. And as Christians, we are part of God's people. We have brothers and sisters in Christ. We have church.

How does church fit into the agenda that God has for each one of us? That's what we'll look at in this session. Let's start by looking at some key Bible passages about church.

2. Bible survey: What's church about?

Divide into subgroups for this exercise if you think that would be useful. Depending on how you are going for time, you might want to divide the passages up amongst the groups.

Do the three summary questions at the end of this section back in the main group.

Timing: 40 minutes

In the New Testament, the Greek word that we translate as 'church' in our English Bibles is *ekklesia*. In the language of the time, it was an everyday word that meant 'gathering' or 'assembly'. So in Acts 19 where there is a riot in the city of Ephesus, the word *ekklesia* is used to describe both the unruly crowd who is outraged by Paul's teaching, and the regular assembly that gets together to discuss civic matters:

> Now some cried out one thing, some another, for the **assembly** was in confusion, and most of them did not know why they had come together. (Acts 19:32)

> If therefore Demetrius and the craftsmen with him have a complaint against anyone, the courts are open, and there are proconsuls. Let them bring charges against one another. [39] But if you seek anything further, it shall be settled in the regular **assembly**. (Acts 19:38-39)

The word translated 'assembly' in these passages is the same one that is translated 'church' in most other passages in the New Testament. The word simply means a gathering, a get-together, an assembly, a congregation.

What we need to investigate then is this: what is the nature of the **Christian** assembly or congregation? What is distinctive about it? Why do Christians gather, and what should Christians do when they are assembled?

Look through the following passages, and write down anything you can discover about the nature of the Christian gathering (or 'church'), and what sorts of things we should do when we gather.

Passage	What is the nature of the Christian assembly?	What should Christians do when they gather?
Matt 16:16-18		
Rom 12:3-8		
1 Cor 1:2		

1 Cor 14:26-33		
Eph 4:11-16		
Col 3:12-17		
1 Tim 4:11-16		
Heb 10:24-25		
Heb 12:18-24		

A. How would you summarize the nature of the Christian gathering?

B. What are the key things we should do when we gather?

3. Input: Understanding church

Play video clip 16 here, or give your own talk based on its content.

Timing: 15 minutes

Script:

You'll have to forgive my perverse sense of humour, but my favourite verse in the New Testament about 'church' is the one from Acts 19:

> Now some cried out one thing, some another, for the congregation was in confusion, and most of them did not know why they had come together. (Acts 19:32)

Now this was a riotous pagan congregation or assembly or 'church' in Ephesus, but it's true that many Christians are in confusion and don't really know why they come together as an assembly or church. People go to church for all sorts of reasons.

- Some go simply out of social custom and habit—because it's the done thing, or because it's what they've always done.
- Others go in order to have a personal experience of God, as if church is a building in which God lives and where you can get in touch with him or receive some sort of blessing.
- Some people go because they think it's a religious duty that God will reward.
- Others go for the experience of the singing and the music, because it lifts their spirits and makes them feel closer to God.
- Others go for the friendship and the relationships, for the social network.

So what does the Bible say about our church gatherings? About what church is for and what we should do when we're together?

It's not the easiest passage to understand at first reading, but Hebrews 12 is a vital passage to study if we're going to grasp what the Bible says about our gatherings—because this passage talks about two gatherings or churches. One is the assembly around Mount Sinai in the Old Testament, where God gave Israel the law. This was the classic assembly or congregation of the Old Testament, where God met with his saved people and spoke to them. And the other assembly in Hebrews 12 is the gathering of the new covenant that is around Jesus in heaven:

> But you have come to Mount Zion and to the city of the living God, the heavenly Jerusalem, and to innumerable angels in festal gathering, [23] and to the assembly of the firstborn who are enrolled in heaven, and to God, the judge of all, and to the spirits of the righteous made perfect, [24] and to Jesus, the mediator of a new covenant, and to the sprinkled blood that speaks a better word than the blood of Abel. (Heb 12:22-24)

How can we be gathered around Jesus in heaven now? I don't know what it's like where you are, but I certainly don't feel I'm in heaven right now.

Well, we already know the answer to this, because we've already looked at this. Let's rewind and play back what we talked in about in seminar 7.

> **[Recap of material in seminar 7:]**
>
> > If then you have been raised with Christ, seek the things that are above, where Christ is, seated at the right hand of God. [2] Set your minds on things that are above, not on things that are on earth. [3] For you have died, and your life is hidden with Christ in God. [4] When Christ who is your life appears, then you also will appear with him in glory. (Col 3:1-4)
>
> Paul says here much of what he said in 2 Corinthians 5—that Christ's death is our death; that we have 'died' with him.
>
> But in this passage he goes further and says that Christ's resurrection is also our resurrection. We **have been raised with Christ**, and our **life is hidden with Christ in God**.
>
> The risen Jesus sits at God's right hand above, and that's where our true life now is. Because we're one with Christ, united with him, then we belong where he is, in his eternal kingdom. Our membership of that kingdom depends entirely on us being 'in him', part of him, united with him by faith, so that where he is, we are also.
>
> But it's a hidden life. It is above. And it will only come into full view on that great day when Jesus comes again in all his glory. And then who we really are, what our life really is, will also be apparent to everyone.

You will also remember the life-changing implication of the fact that we are now raised up with Christ, and that our true life is hidden there with him. It's to put sin to death now in our lives, and to clothe ourselves with Christ's character—not in order to get to heaven, but because we are already there in Christ. Because we are raised with Christ above, we need to live that way. The old self is dead and gone—so we must get rid of anything that belongs to that old life, and put on what belongs to the new life.

Well, all Hebrews 12 is saying is that none of this takes place in isolation. There's a whole crowd or assembly or church of us who are united with Christ, who are members of his eternal kingdom, and whose lives are hidden with Christ in God.

And there's a whole crowd or assembly of people here on earth who, as a consequence, are striving to put sin to death and clothe themselves with the character of Christ.

When we are united with Christ, we are also united with a great family of brothers and sisters who just like us are enrolled in heaven, and just like us are striving to move step by step towards maturity in Christ.

And that's what our local church gatherings are, and what they are for. They are gatherings of God's redeemed and transferred people here and now. Christ is there in the midst of the gathering, speaking his Word, and we are all there to shepherd each other towards maturity in Christ.

A few pages earlier in Hebrews, that's exactly what the writer urges us to do when we gather:

> And let us consider how to stir up one another to love and good works, [25] not neglecting to meet together, as is the habit of some, but encouraging one another, and all the more as you see the Day drawing near. (Heb 10:24-25)

It's also what Paul says as he writes to the somewhat wayward Corinthians and urges them to get their chaotic church meetings back on track. The key thing, he keeps saying, is building each other up. Whatever you do, let everything be for edification, for building, for encouragement, for growth in Christlikeness.

In other words, church is a bunch of people who are all pursuing God's agenda **together**; who meet together to push each other forwards to maturity in Christ.

We often think of church in terms of what we get out of it. We come home some Sundays thinking (somewhat grumpily), "Well, that wasn't a very good sermon. I didn't get much out of that." Or "I didn't find the music inspiring **at all**". Or whatever (or whoever!) else it is that doesn't impress us.

But that's not why we go to church. We go in order to build. We go in order to share together in the basic task of the Christian life, which is to push ourselves and others forward step by step towards maturity in Christ.

4. Implications

Talk these questions through in the whole group.

Timing: 20 minutes

A. If this is the biblical vision of church, practically speaking what should we do when we gather as a church?

B. Does what we have seen in this session challenge your own attitudes about church? If so, how?

C. When you're in your church gatherings, what could you do to encourage others and help them to move forward in Christ?

(i) Before you get there

(ii) During the main part of the meeting

(iii) As you chat afterwards

D. Pray for your church.

Part 6: Reflect, share, pray

About this session

This final session provides an opportunity for personal reflection and group sharing. It starts with time for people to reflect seriously about their lives and about the implications of what they have been learning, and then moves on to a chance for them to share some of those thoughts with the group as a whole.

1. Reflect

Encourage the participants to find somewhere quiet on their own and to think and pray seriously about their lives, using the questions below as a stimulus.

Timing: 30-40 minutes

Here's the *Course of Your Life* summary that we've been working on:

Because God's agenda is
- **to transfer us into Christ's kingdom**
- **and to transform us to be like Christ**

then our agenda is
- **to press forward towards maturity in Christ by prayerfully setting our minds on God's word**
- **and to move others towards maturity in Christ by prayerfully speaking God's word to them.**

Spend some time on your own thinking about the following questions, and then praying about what you've written.

A. Where are you up to in growing towards maturity in Christ? Are there areas in which you have been particularly challenged this weekend?

B. What are the next steps for you personally in pressing towards maturity in Christ? Which of these steps will be hardest?

C. Think about the people in your life: at home, at work, in your family, in your friendship networks, and at church. Who do you want to move towards Christ and towards maturity in him? Be a bit specific. Write down one or two names in each area, and think of some things you could do for each person.

	Name	How could I move them forwards?
Home		
Work		

Family		
Friends		
Church		

D. Think about the overall shape of your life. How might advancing God's agenda reorder the priorities and structures in your life?

E. What's the simple, no-brainer thing that you could implement as a result of what you have learned in this intensive?

F. Be ready to share: in the next section, you'll each have an opportunity to encourage others in the group by sharing some of the things you've written down above. You might like to tell the group:

- the thing that challenged you most in this intensive

- the changes you'll find hardest to make

- the steps you'd like to take in helping others move towards maturity in Christ

- or something else entirely!

2. Share and pray

To round off the intensive, go around the whole group and give each person an opportunity to share some of their personal reflections. Then have someone else in the group pray for them.

Timing: 30-40 minutes

Seminar 9
Where to now?

About this seminar

The purpose of this final seminar is partly to summarize and draw together the content of the course—although much of that work has already been done during the intensive.

The more important aspect of this seminar is to think about the future. How will what we've learned play out in our lives in the weeks and months and years to come?

What you organize in terms of follow-up will depend on how you are running the course. If, as we recommend, you run it as part of a group that will continue to meet together (as a Bible study group, for example), then following up on the course will be part of your ongoing life together.

However, if participants will not be continuing to meet together regularly, you will want to work out a way to keep in touch and keep the momentum going. There are plenty of things you could do. For example:

- Send an encouraging group email every week or two (e.g. with snippets and reminders from the course material).
- Continue to share prayer points (e.g. by email), especially praying for those people you are seeking to help move forward in Christ.
- Continue to gather once a month for prayer and mutual support in putting the principles into effect.
- Organize a group reunion in three months' time.
- Work on an evangelistic activity together—for example, inviting the

non-Christian friends you are praying for to an informal discussion evening about Christianity.

In many ways, you (as course leader) need to work out how to implement the very principles we've been examining—that is, how you can continue to help all the participants to keep moving forward, one step at a time, to maturity in Christ. And the next step for many of them will be to work out who they want to start reading the Bible with (their housemate, their spouse, their children, their friends).

1. Discussion: Heads, hearts and hands

Start in subgroups of four or five for this discussion.

Timing: 30 minutes

As we look back over all that we've learned and all that we've done, one way to draw it together is to say that we have been addressing our heads, hearts and hands. Let's start by talking about our heads and our hearts.

A. Heads

We've covered a lot of Bible material during our time together. We could summarize much of it with the statement that we've been looking at in seminar 8 and during the intensive:

Because God's agenda is
- **to transfer us into Christ's kingdom**
- **and to transform us to be like Christ**

then our agenda is
- **to press forward towards maturity in Christ by prayerfully setting our minds on God's word**
- **and to move others towards maturity in Christ by prayerfully speaking God's word to them.**

Looking back over the **content** of the course, what have you learned that is new or striking? How has your understanding or knowledge grown—about God and his plans, and about yourself and your life?

B. Hearts

This understanding of what God wants us to do with the rest of our lives is very challenging. It confronts and opposes the worldly goals and priorities that most of us have in our hearts.

- How has the course challenged your priorities and goals in life? In what ways has your heart been changed?

- What are the areas of sin in your life that you've been challenged about during the course? What do you need to "put to death"? What aspects of Christlikeness do you especially need to adopt?

C. Prayer

We'll come back to our 'hands' below. But first, spend some time praying in your groups about the matters you've shared.

2. Input: Where to from here?

Play video clip 12 here, or give your own short talk based on its content.

Timing: 7 minutes

Script:

Several weeks ago, we set out on a search for answers to some massive questions. Why am I here? What is my life really about? Is it going anywhere? Does the God who created me have some sort of purpose for the course of my life? And if so, how does that translate into the next week, the next month, the next years of my life?

And I warned you that as a result of what we found, your life might never be the same again.

My prayer and hope and trust is that your life **will** never be the same again. I hope you have been gripped afresh—or perhaps for the first time—by the cosmic, history-wide, awe-inspiring plans of God for our world, and for each one of us. I hope you have grasped something of what God has done in Christ, and what his purposes are in Christ, and what that means for every aspect of your life, and I hope this has revolutionized your vision of what your life is about.

In particular, my prayer is that everyone who does this course will have a clearer grasp of what it means for us to die with Christ, and to be raised up with him, and now to live a completely new life—a life in which we put to death the sin that still clings to us, and clothe ourselves instead with the character of our Lord. I pray that you will never again be complacent about the sin in your life, but that you will cast it off with all the passion and vehemence with which you might rid yourself of a disease or a filthy garment.

And as you seek to press forward towards maturity in Christ, I pray that part of your growing Christlikeness will be a shepherd's heart that longs to move others forward as well; to move them one step forwards towards Christ, no matter where they are on the spectrum.

We are often tempted to think that the next thing God wants us to do involves a grand plan of some sort; that if we're going to contribute to the work of his kingdom it will mean signing up for something at church, or putting on an impressive event that you invite lots of people to. And these things are all good.

But truthfully, **the next step is a person**—because that's how it happens: one person at a time. That's what we talked about during the intensive. The next step is for you to prayerfully consider who you could shepherd towards maturity in Christ by prayerfully speaking God's word to them in some way.

And then the next step after that is… another step forward for that person, or for another person.

Way back in seminar 1, you considered those people who have been most influential in the course of your life. It's now time to think about that question in reverse: who are the people in whose lives you are going to be influential? Who are you going to move forward? Who are you going to shepherd forward towards Christ?

One of the really handy things about this course is that you've already learned how to do this. You've read the Bible with someone nine or ten times, using a variety of methods. And although there are many, many ways in which we can share a word with someone for their benefit, one of the easiest and most effective is simply to open the Bible and read it together.

Before we go any further, why don't you pause and talk together about the one-to-one Bible readings you've been doing.

3. Getting our hands dirty

Break into pairs for this (not with your regular one-to-one partner).

Timing: 20 minutes

Over the duration of the course, we've addressed our heads and our hearts, but also our hands. We've learned a practical skill—that is, how to read the Bible one-to-one with someone else.

- How did you feel about the one-to-one meetings before you started them? What have you learned along the way?

- What was your favourite method of reading one-to-one—question and answer, the Swedish method or COMA?

- Think about who you might invite to read the Bible with you—for example, a Christian friend at church, a non-Christian friend, your housemate, your spouse, your kids. Jot down some possibilities.

- Pray together that God would open the way for you to start a Bible reading partnership with someone in the next month.

A useful resource

To consolidate what you've learned about one-to-one Bible reading, get yourself a copy of *One-to-One Bible Reading: a simple guide for every Christian* by David Helm.[6] It not only summarizes very neatly what you've been learning, but also gives lots of really useful suggestions about what to read with different people, and how to approach the different kinds of writing in the Bible

6   Matthias Media, Sydney, 2011

(e.g. letters, poetry, narrative, prophecy, etc.). It's an excellent little tool, especially for those who lack confidence in reading the Bible with others.

4. The freedom of the future

Come back together as one group. If you think you have time, kick this final section off by asking people to share some of what they learned through doing the one-to-one readings together.

Timing: 20 minutes

The glorious thing about the course of our lives is that God gives us an agenda, but not a detailed script. We don't know all the details of how we are going to live out God's agenda in every aspect of our lives.

What we do know is that we don't embark on this adventure alone. God is with us by his Spirit as we encourage one another, share ideas, work in harness together, and pray for each other.

Conclude your time together by doing four things:

- Brainstorm together about all the different ways you could cooperate and help each other to advance God's agenda in the world. How could you help each other in moving people towards maturity in Christ? See how many ideas you can come up with.
- Talk together about how to follow through on the gains made in this course. How are you going to keep encouraging each other? When are you going to meet again in order to talk and pray about how you're all going?
- Quickly look through appendix 1, or watch the video clip 'Matthias Media and God's agenda' (on the course DVD under 'Extra videos'). This provides a quick introduction to the many useful resources Matthias Media produces to help you pursue God's agenda.
- Pray as a group, giving thanks for all that you've learned, and asking God to bless your plans and efforts by his Spirit.

One-to-one meetings

Introduction

The Course of Your Life basically revolves around reading, studying, exploring and absorbing God's word—and being profoundly challenged and changed by what we find there.

However, in his wise and gracious way, God has given us not only his word (in the Bible), but also each other. We are able to learn from each other, to be challenged and pushed by each other, and to pray for each other.

The one-to-one component of *The Course of Your Life* brings these two gifts of God together in a simple, powerful way: two people reading the Bible together, helping each other to see what God is saying there, and praying for each other that you might obey what you hear.

Here are some simple guidelines to help you make the most of your one-to-one meetings:

1. **Find a mutually convenient time** that you can use as your regular meeting time for the duration of the course—over breakfast, at lunchtime, after work, on Sunday afternoons, or whenever. Your course leader has tried to pair you with someone who either lives or works relatively close to you, to make the process easier.

2. **There is no preparation** to be done before you get together. The personal readings that you do on your own will relate to the one-to-one meetings, but there is no formal 'homework' or set reading to do before you get together.

3. **There is no leader.** You are just two people getting together to help each other learn from the Bible.

4. Try to keep your one-to-one meetings to **under an hour**. Here's a suggested time frame for each of your meetings:
   - 5 mins: chat, get some coffee, talk about how you're going.
   - 10 mins: share one thing each that you'd like to give thanks for, and one thing each that you'd like to pray for. Then pray together. If you meet together in a place where praying feels awkward, try to find a better place! If that's not possible then just keep your prayers brief, and commit to pray for each other later on your own.
   - 30 mins: read the passage together (perhaps reading aloud half each) and then talk through what it means, and how it applies to your lives.
   - 5 mins: finish with prayer arising from the passage.

5. **Have conversations, not monologues.** The idea is to hear what God is saying in the Bible. Try to avoid giving your opinions at length, or getting on to your hobbyhorses.

6. **Don't be afraid to ask questions.** If you notice something that you don't understand or that doesn't seem to make sense, don't gloss over it. Focus in on it. See if you can answer it by looking more closely, especially at the rest of the passage. (It's very often by unlocking the things we don't really understand in a passage that the whole thing starts to make sense.)

7. For some of you, meeting one-to-one to read the Bible will be **a new experience**. To make it as simple as possible for you to get started, we've provided guidelines for each meeting (questions to answer, exercises related to the passage). Don't feel limited or constrained by the questions. They are there to stimulate your discussion together about the passage. As you go along, you may find that you don't really need to stick to the suggested questions or lines of enquiry, and that you'd prefer to delve into the passage in your own way. Go for it!

One other thing: you'll notice that we've printed out the passage for study. This not only makes it easy for you to take just this booklet with you to your one-to-one meetings, but it also ensures that you both have the same Bible translation in front of you. This makes reading the Bible together much easier!

One-to-one meeting 1

Colossians 1:1-14

1. Give yourselves a few minutes to settle in, get some food and drink (if appropriate), and chat. Share one thing each that you'd like to give thanks for to God, and one thing that you're anxious about and would like to bring before God in prayer. Then pray for each other.

2. Read Colossians 1:1-14 together.

Paul, an apostle of Christ Jesus by the will of God, and Timothy our brother,

2 To the saints and faithful brothers in Christ at Colossae:

Grace to you and peace from God our Father.

3 We always thank God, the Father of our Lord Jesus Christ, when we pray for you, 4 since we heard of your faith in Christ Jesus and of the love that you have for all the saints, 5 because of the hope laid up for you in heaven. Of this you have heard before in the word of the truth, the gospel, 6 which has come to you, as indeed in the whole world it is bearing fruit and increasing—as it also does among you, since the day you heard it and understood the grace of God in truth, 7 just as you learned it from Epaphras our beloved fellow servant. He is a faithful minister of Christ on your behalf 8 and has made known to us your love in the Spirit.

9 And so, from the day we heard, we have not ceased to pray for you, asking that you may be filled with the knowledge of his will in all spiritual wisdom and understanding, 10 so as to walk in a manner worthy of the Lord, fully pleasing to him, bearing fruit in every good work and increasing in the knowledge of God. 11 May you be strengthened with all power, according to his glorious might, for all endurance and patience with joy, 12 giving thanks to the Father, who has qualified you to share in the inheritance of the saints in light. 13 He has delivered us from the domain of darkness and transferred us to the kingdom of his beloved Son, 14 in whom we have redemption, the forgiveness of sins.

3. Note down everything the passage says about:

- things that are past tense; things that happened in the past

- things that are in the present experience of the Colossians

- things that will happen in the future

4. Looking again over the passage, what do we learn about "the gospel"?

- Its content

- What it produces or achieves

5. Implications:

- When did the "word of the truth" first come into your life? What fruit do you think it has borne in and through you?

- What does this passage stimulate you to give thanks for, and to pray for?

6. Finish with thanksgiving and prayer.

One-to-one meeting 2

Colossians 1:15-20

1. After you've given yourselves a few minutes to settle in, get some food and chat, share one thing each that you'd like to thank God for, and one thing each that you're anxious about and would like to bring before God in prayer. Then pray for each other.

2. The questions below focus on verses 15-20, but to get the flow of things, read through Colossians 1:11-20.

> May you be strengthened with all power, according to his glorious might, for all endurance and patience with joy, [12] giving thanks to the Father, who has qualified you to share in the inheritance of the saints in light. [13] He has delivered us from the domain of darkness and transferred us to the kingdom of his beloved Son, [14] in whom we have redemption, the forgiveness of sins.
>   [15] He is the image of the invisible God, the firstborn of all creation. [16] For by him all things were created, in heaven and on earth, visible and invisible, whether thrones or dominions or rulers or authorities—all things were created through him and for him. [17] And he is before all things, and in him all things hold together. [18] And he is the head of the body, the church. He is the beginning, the firstborn from the dead, that in everything he might be preeminent. [19] For in him all the fullness of God was pleased to dwell, [20] and through him to reconcile to himself all things, whether on earth or in heaven, making peace by the blood of his cross.

3. See if you can work out the logic of verses 15-20 by looking for the main connecting words (like 'for', 'and', but', 'that', etc.).

4. Write down everything that describes the relationship between the Son and:
- God

- all created things

- the church

(Tip: the term 'firstborn' in verses 15 and 18 basically means 'heir'. The firstborn son in the ancient world was the sole inheritor of his father's possessions. To be the 'firstborn' was to be one who inherited everything.)

5. Implications:
- According to this passage, what is the purpose of all created things? What does this mean for your own life?

- What does this passage stimulate you to give thanks for, and to pray for?

6. Finish with thanksgiving and prayer.

One-to-one meeting 3

Colossians 1:19-23

1. After you've given yourselves a few minutes to settle in, get some food and chat, share one thing each that you'd like to thank God for, and one thing each that you're anxious about and would like to bring before God in prayer. Then pray for each other.

2. Read through Colossians 1:19-29.

> For in him all the fullness of God was pleased to dwell, [20] and through him to reconcile to himself all things, whether on earth or in heaven, making peace by the blood of his cross.
>
> [21] And you, who once were alienated and hostile in mind, doing evil deeds, [22] he has now reconciled in his body of flesh by his death, in order to present you holy and blameless and above reproach before him, [23] if indeed you continue in the faith, stable and steadfast, not shifting from the hope of the gospel that you heard, which has been proclaimed in all creation under heaven, and of which I, Paul, became a minister.
>
> [24] Now I rejoice in my sufferings for your sake, and in my flesh I am filling up what is lacking in Christ's afflictions for the sake of his body, that is, the church, [25] of which I became a minister according to the stewardship from God that was given to me for you, to make the word of God fully known, [26] the mystery hidden for ages and generations but now revealed to his saints. [27] To them God chose to make known how great among the Gentiles are the riches of the glory of this mystery, which is Christ in you, the hope of glory. [28] Him we proclaim, warning everyone and teaching everyone with all wisdom, that we may present everyone mature in Christ. [29] For this I toil, struggling with all his energy that he powerfully works within me.

3. What were the Colossians once like? What used to be their relationship to God?

4. Because of something that God has done, the situation or status of the Colossians has changed.

- What has changed? How is their situation different? (Compare Colossians 1:13—"He has delivered us from the domain of darkness and transferred us to the kingdom of his beloved Son".)

- How did this change come about? How was it achieved?

- What is the purpose or end result of this change?

5. What does this passage say about the role and response of the Colossians?

6. Implications:

- How do you see enmity or hostility to God expressed in the world around you?

- Thinking back over Colossians 1, where in the chapter do you see the theme of endurance or perseverance in Christ?

- What does this passage stimulate you to give thanks for, and to pray for?

7. Finish with thanksgiving and prayer.

One-to-one meeting 4

Colossians 1:24-2:5

1. Share with one another how you are going, and then pray briefly for each other and for your time together reading the Bible.

2. In this one-to-one meeting, you're going to try a slightly different way of reading the Bible together. It's called 'the Swedish method' (after the nationality of the person who made it popular), and it's very straightforward. You simply read the passage and then jot down some notes under three categories:

 A light bulb: anything that stands out in the passage as you read it—such as repeated words or phrases, or particularly striking ideas.

 A question mark: something that you don't understand or that puzzles you.

 An arrow: something that applies personally to your life.

Start by reading the passage: Colossians 1:24-2:5.

> Now I rejoice in my sufferings for your sake, and in my flesh I am filling up what is lacking in Christ's afflictions for the sake of his body, that is, the church, [25] of which I became a minister according to the stewardship from God that was given to me for you, to make the word of God fully known, [26] the mystery hidden for ages and generations but now revealed to his saints. [27] To them God chose to make known how great among the Gentiles are the riches of the glory of this mystery, which is Christ in you, the hope of glory. [28] Him we proclaim, warning everyone and teaching everyone with all wisdom, that we may present everyone mature in Christ. [29] For this I toil, struggling with all his energy that he powerfully works within me.
>
> [2:1] For I want you to know how great a struggle I have for you and for those at Laodicea and for all who have not seen me face to face,

[2] that their hearts may be encouraged, being knit together in love, to reach all the riches of full assurance of understanding and the knowledge of God's mystery, which is Christ, [3] in whom are hidden all the treasures of wisdom and knowledge. [4] I say this in order that no-one may delude you with plausible arguments. [5] For though I am absent in body, yet I am with you in spirit, rejoicing to see your good order and the firmness of your faith in Christ.

3. Now jot down one or two things next to each symbol below. Take a couple of minutes to do this on your own, and then:

- share your light bulbs with each other
- share your questions with each other (and see if you can come up with any answers)
- share your arrows with each other.

4. Finish with thanksgiving and prayer based on what you have learned and shared together from this passage.

One-to-one meeting 5

Colossians 2:6-15

1. Share with one another how you are going, and then pray briefly for each other and for your time together reading the Bible.

2. Read Colossians 2:6-15 and talk about it together using the Swedish method.

> Therefore, as you received Christ Jesus the Lord, so walk in him, [7] rooted and built up in him and established in the faith, just as you were taught, abounding in thanksgiving.
> [8] See to it that no-one takes you captive by philosophy and empty deceit, according to human tradition, according to the elemental spirits of the world, and not according to Christ. [9] For in him the whole fullness of deity dwells bodily, [10] and you have been filled in him, who is the head of all rule and authority. [11] In him also you were circumcised with a circumcision made without hands, by putting off the body of the flesh, by the circumcision of Christ, [12] having been buried with him in baptism, in which you were also raised with him through faith in the powerful working of God, who raised him from the dead. [13] And you, who were dead in your trespasses and the uncircumcision of your flesh, God made alive together with him, having forgiven us all our trespasses, [14] by cancelling the record of debt that stood against us with its legal demands. This he set aside, nailing it to the cross. [15] He disarmed the rulers and authorities and put them to open shame, by triumphing over them in him.

3. Jot down one or two things next to each symbol below. Take a couple of minutes to do this on your own, and then:
- share your light bulbs with each other
- share your questions with each other (and see if you can come up with any answers)
- share your arrows with each other.

4. Finish with thanksgiving and prayer based on what you have learned and shared together from this passage.

One-to-one meeting 6

Colossians 2:16-23

1. Share with one another how you are going, and then pray briefly for each other and for your time together reading the Bible.

2. Read Colossians 2:16-23 and talk about it together using the Swedish method.

> Therefore let no-one pass judgment on you in questions of food and drink, or with regard to a festival or a new moon or a Sabbath. ¹⁷ These are a shadow of the things to come, but the substance belongs to Christ. ¹⁸ Let no-one disqualify you, insisting on asceticism and worship of angels, going on in detail about visions, puffed up without reason by his sensuous mind, ¹⁹ and not holding fast to the Head, from whom the whole body, nourished and knit together through its joints and ligaments, grows with a growth that is from God.
>
> ²⁰ If with Christ you died to the elemental spirits of the world, why, as if you were still alive in the world, do you submit to regulations— ²¹ "Do not handle, Do not taste, Do not touch" ²² (referring to things that all perish as they are used)—according to human precepts and teachings? ²³ These have indeed an appearance of wisdom in promoting self-made religion and asceticism and severity to the body, but they are of no value in stopping the indulgence of the flesh.

3. Jot down one or two things next to each symbol below. Take a couple of minutes to do this on your own, and then:
- share your light bulbs with each other
- share your questions with each other (and see if you can come up with any answers)
- share your arrows with each other.

4. Finish with thanksgiving and prayer based on what you have learned and shared together from this passage.

One-to-one meeting 7

Colossians 3:1-4

1. Share with one another how you are going, and then pray briefly for each other and for your time together reading the Bible.

2. So far in your one-to-one meetings, you've used questions and answers (meetings 1-3), and the Swedish method (meetings 4-6). Now you're going try another way of reading the Bible together. It's called COMA, which stands for **c**ontext, **o**bservation, **m**eaning and **a**pplication. Start by reading Colossians 3:1-4.

> If then you have been raised with Christ, seek the things that are above, where Christ is, seated at the right hand of God. ² Set your minds on things that are above, not on things that are on earth. ³ For you have died, and your life is hidden with Christ in God. ⁴ When Christ who is your life appears, then you also will appear with him in glory.

3. Now read back over the passage and see what you can jot down together under the four COMA headings.

Context:
- Where is Paul up to in his argument? What has he just said in the previous few paragraphs?

Observation:

- Are there any major subsections or breaks in the text?
- What are the most important words or phrases? What is the main point or points?
- What surprises are there?

Meaning:

- How does this text relate to other parts of the book?
- How does the passage relate to Jesus?
- What does this teach you about God?
- How could you sum up the meaning of this passage in your own words?

Application:

- How does this passage challenge your understanding?
- Is there some attitude you need to change?
- How does this passage call on you to change the way you live?

4. Give thanks and pray based on what you have learned.

One-to-one meeting 8

Colossians 3:5-17

1. Share with one another how you are going, and then pray briefly for each other and for your time together reading the Bible.

2. Read Colossians 3:5-17.

> Put to death therefore what is earthly in you: sexual immorality, impurity, passion, evil desire, and covetousness, which is idolatry. ⁶ On account of these the wrath of God is coming. ⁷ In these you too once walked, when you were living in them. ⁸ But now you must put them all away: anger, wrath, malice, slander, and obscene talk from your mouth. ⁹ Do not lie to one another, seeing that you have put off the old self with its practices ¹⁰ and have put on the new self, which is being renewed in knowledge after the image of its creator. ¹¹ Here there is not Greek and Jew, circumcised and uncircumcised, barbarian, Scythian, slave, free; but Christ is all, and in all.
>
> ¹² Put on then, as God's chosen ones, holy and beloved, compassionate hearts, kindness, humility, meekness, and patience, ¹³ bearing with one another and, if one has a complaint against another, forgiving each other; as the Lord has forgiven you, so you also must forgive. ¹⁴ And above all these put on love, which binds everything together in perfect harmony. ¹⁵ And let the peace of Christ rule in your hearts, to which indeed you were called in one body. And be thankful. ¹⁶ Let the word of Christ dwell in you richly, teaching and admonishing one another in all wisdom, singing psalms and hymns and spiritual songs, with thankfulness in your hearts to God. ¹⁷ And whatever you do, in word or deed, do everything in the name of the Lord Jesus, giving thanks to God the Father through him.

3. Now read back over the passage and see what you can jot down together under the four COMA headings.

Context:

- Where is Paul up to in his argument? What has he just said in the previous few paragraphs?

Observation:

- Are there any major subsections or breaks in the text?
- What are the most important words or phrases? What is the main point or points?
- What surprises are there?

Meaning:

- How does this text relate to other parts of the book?
- How does the passage relate to Jesus?
- What does this teach you about God?
- How could you sum up the meaning of this passage in your own words?

Application:

- How does this passage challenge your understanding?
- Is there some attitude you need to change?
- How does this passage call on you to change the way you live?

4. Give thanks and pray based on what you have learned.

One-to-one meeting 9

Colossians 3:17-4:1

1. Share one thing each that you'd like to thank God for, and one thing each that you would like to bring before God in prayer. Then pray for each other.

2. Read Colossians 3:17-4:1 through twice.

> And whatever you do, in word or deed, do everything in the name of the Lord Jesus, giving thanks to God the Father through him.
> [18] Wives, submit to your husbands, as is fitting in the Lord. [19] Husbands, love your wives, and do not be harsh with them. [20] Children, obey your parents in everything, for this pleases the Lord. [21] Fathers, do not provoke your children, lest they become discouraged. [22] Bondservants, obey in everything those who are your earthly masters, not by way of eye-service, as people-pleasers, but with sincerity of heart, fearing the Lord. [23] Whatever you do, work heartily, as for the Lord and not for men, [24] knowing that from the Lord you will receive the inheritance as your reward. You are serving the Lord Christ. [25] For the wrongdoer will be paid back for the wrong he has done, and there is no partiality.
> [4:1] Masters, treat your bondservants justly and fairly, knowing that you also have a Master in heaven.

3. Without using any particular framework or method, talk together about what you think this passage is saying—its key points, its logic, its main idea—and then also talk about how it applies to your life. Jot down the key things you discover together, and then pray about them.

One-to-one meeting 10

Colossians 4:2-6

1. Share one thing each that you'd like to thank God for, and one thing each that you would like to bring before God in prayer. Then pray for each other.

2. Read Colossians 4:2-6 through twice.

> Continue steadfastly in prayer, being watchful in it with thanksgiving. [3] At the same time, pray also for us, that God may open to us a door for the word, to declare the mystery of Christ, on account of which I am in prison—[4] that I may make it clear, which is how I ought to speak.
> [5] Walk in wisdom toward outsiders, making the best use of the time. [6] Let your speech always be gracious, seasoned with salt, so that you may know how you ought to answer each person.

3. Without using any particular framework or method, talk together about what you think this passage is saying—its key points, its logic, its main idea—and then also talk about how it applies to your life. Jot down the key things you discover together, and then pray about them.

Appendix 1

Matthias Media and God's agenda

During this course we've developed a summary of God's agenda for the course of our lives. This is how we put it:

> **Because God's agenda is**
> - **to transfer us into Christ's kingdom**
> - **and to transform us to be like Christ**
>
> **then our agenda is**
> - **to press forward towards maturity in Christ by prayerfully setting our minds on God's word**
> - **and to move others towards maturity in Christ by prayerfully speaking God's word to them.**

Our mission at Matthias Media is basically to produce resources of all kinds that equip Christians to pursue God's agenda in their lives—to grow to maturity in Christ, and to minister to others to see them grow to maturity in Christ as well.

Below are listed some of our most popular and useful resources that can help you in pursuing God's agenda. For more details about these resources and many others, visit our website: **www.matthiasmedia.com**

Resources to help you press forward to maturity in Christ

The Briefing

Matthias Media has been publishing *The Briefing* in various formats for more than two decades. It's now available as a free online web magazine, as well as in a full-colour paper edition published six times a year and available by subscription. In *The Briefing* you'll find:

- Articles, audio and video to help Christians grow in their knowledge of God, and in their passion for godliness day by day.
- Ideas and examples to encourage all Christians in helping others grow towards maturity in Christ.
- A Christian perspective on the ideas and events of the world around us (including book reviews).
- Resources and ideas for pastors and other full-time gospel workers as they lead God's people in serving him.

For more information, visit the website: **matthiasmedia.com/briefing**

The Daily Reading Bible

The Daily Reading Bible is an all-in-one resource that helps you set your mind every day on God's word in the Bible.

Each volume contains around 60 undated readings. Each reading is designed to take around 15-20 minutes, and contains:

- the full text of the Bible passage for that reading
- some questions to get you thinking
- some 'points to ponder'
- some ideas to get you started in prayer.

It's all in one booklet that you can take with you anywhere—on the train, on the bus, to the park at lunchtime, or to your favourite armchair.

Guidebooks for Life

This is a series of straightforward, practical books that deal with the important nuts-and-bolts topics that Christians need to know about as we walk each day with our Master. Some Christian books are all theory and no practical application; others are all stories and tips with no substance. The Guidebooks for Life aim to achieve a vital balance—that is, to dig into the Bible and discover what God is telling us there, as well as apply that truth to our daily lives.

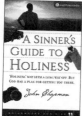

Key titles in the series include:

- *A Sinner's Guide to Holiness*, by John Chapman
- *Guidance and the Voice of God*, by Phillip Jensen and Tony Payne
- *Encouragement: How words change lives*, by Gordon Cheng

Resources to help you move others forward to maturity in Christ

Towards the end of *The Course of Your Life* we looked at the following diagram, which helps us to visualize our goal of helping others move forward, step by step, towards maturity in Christ:

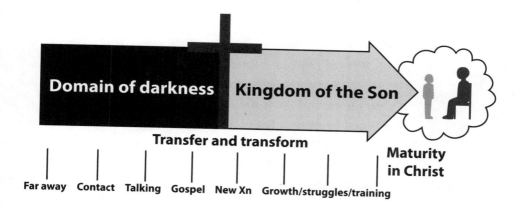

At Matthias Media, we divide all our resources into four categories that reflect this continuum of growth towards Christ:

- **Outreach**: talking about spiritual issues with our friends, and sharing the gospel with them
- **Follow-up**: establishing new and young Christians in the kingdom
- **Growth**: putting sin to death, and clothing ourselves with Christ's character
- **Training**: learning to serve others in **outreach**, **follow-up** and **growth**

Here are some of our key resources in each category.

Resources for outreach

The Essential Jesus

This innovative 80-page book combines a fresh translation of Luke's Gospel with an introduction and conclusion based on the well-known *Two Ways to Live* framework. The result is a very economical and effective way to share the gospel with lots of people.

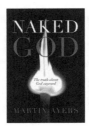

Naked God

In *Naked God*, former lawyer Martin Ayers provides an opportunity for interested enquirers to examine the big questions: Is there a God? How can I know the truth given that different religions make different claims? And if there is a God, what real difference will he make to my life?

Two Ways to Live

Two Ways to Live is a memorable summary of the gospel that has been used to share the gospel with hundreds of thousands of people around the world. It comes in a range of styles, formats and languages, but each different resource that uses the *Two Ways to Live* framework features the same six-step logical presentation of what the Bible says about Jesus Christ. For more information, visit the website: **twowaystolive.com**

Resources for follow-up

Just for Starters

Used by thousands of churches worldwide, *Just for Starters* is widely regarded as **the** Bible study for following up new Christians. The seven studies look at what the Bible teaches on seven fundamental topics: Saved by God, Trusting in God, Living God's way, Listening to God, Talking to God, Meeting with God's family, Meeting the world.

There is a second set of studies in the series as well, called *Christian Living for Starters*.

Right Side Up

This recent book by Paul Grimmond is especially designed for new Christians, to orient them to the new life they have embarked upon with Christ. It not only clearly explains the gospel (so that the foundations are solid), but also goes on to discuss the many practical issues and challenges that new believers face. It's a warm-hearted, engaging, exciting read about the adventure of the Christian life, and as such is a very helpful as a refresher for longer-serving Christians as well.

Resources for growth

Bible studies

We have two main series of Bible studies:
- Pathway Bible Guides: short, simple Bible studies that are easy to digest
- Interactive Bible Studies: solid food for more established Christians

Both series are designed mainly for small groups, although the Pathway series is also very suitable for one-to-one Bible study.

Although pitched at slightly different levels, both series focus closely on the passage of Scripture rather than bouncing too quickly into discussion or application; both seek to read the passage in its context; and both maintain a balance between providing input and direction, and allowing plenty of room for exploration and discovery.

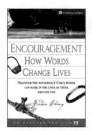

Guidebooks for Life (with discussion guides)

Like many of our resources, the Guidebooks for Life series (described earlier) is not only excellent for seeking to grow ourselves; it is also an excellent tool for helping others grow. Get together with a friend (or in your small home group) and decide to read through one of these helpful books together, using the supplied discussion guide to stimulate your conversation together.

Resources for training

One-to-One Bible Reading: a simple guide for every Christian

You have already begun to learn about one-to-one Bible reading just by doing *The Course of Your Life*. This short, practical and very helpful book by David Helm will train you to take that ministry further. It provides lots of useful ideas about how to start reading the Bible with someone (whether Christian or non-Christian), along with a large range of resources and methods for reading different parts of the Bible. This is a supremely useful little book.

Two Ways to Live training

Our best-known training program is *Two Ways to Live: Know and share the gospel*. This seven-session course teaches participants to know the gospel thoroughly for themselves, and then trains them in how to explain that message clearly and naturally in their own words, using the well-known *Two Ways to Live* framework. With role-plays, DVD and audio input, the course is easy to run and highly effective.

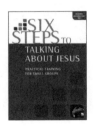

Six Steps courses

The other main plank in our training resources is the DVD-based Six Steps range, now with three titles in the series. Each one contains simple, straightforward training for every Christian in a basic area of Christian living and ministry:
- *Six Steps to Encouragement*: how to encourage one another with God's word
- *Six Steps to Talking About Jesus*: how to begin to share your faith with others
- *Six Steps to Reading your Bible*: how to dig into God's word for yourself

These courses are ideal for running in existing small groups as a framework for training people in knowledge, godliness and the ability to speak God's word to others for their growth in Christ.

Appendix 2

Suggestions for ongoing training

If (as we recommend) you choose to run *The Course of Your Life* as part of an ongoing effort to disciple and train a small group of people, here are some suggestions for using other resources from Matthias Media to construct an extended training program.

Option 1

Training a group for one year (= approximately 40 weeks of content):

Matthias Media Resource	Description	Weeks
The Course of Your Life	A DVD-based course that revolutionizes people's mindset and gives basic training in one-to-one Bible reading	10
Full of Promise	A set of studies that provides an overview and framework for understanding the whole Old Testament	8
Two Ways to Live: Know and share the gospel	A course that teaches participants to know the gospel thoroughly themselves, and then be able to explain it naturally in their own words	7
The Blueprint	A set of studies that provides an overview of key topics in Christian doctrine	10

Option 2

Similar to option 1, but taking longer to work through *The Course of Your Life*:

Matthias Media Resource	Description	Weeks
The Course of Your Life	A DVD-based course that revolutionizes people's mindset and gives basic training in one-to-one Bible reading	18

Full of Promise	A set of studies that provides an overview and framework for understanding the whole Old Testament	8
Six Steps to Talking About Jesus	A DVD-based course that provides a simple introduction to sharing your faith with others (shorter and a bit less demanding than *Two Ways to Live*)	6
Peace with God	A simple set of studies that looks at the most important passages in Paul's majestic letter to the Romans	9

Mix and match

Here are some other useful resources that you could mix and match in options 1 or 2:

Matthias Media Resource	Description	Weeks
Six Steps to Reading Your Bible	A DVD-based course that equips participants with basic skills in reading the Bible for themselves	6
Six Steps to Encouragement	A DVD-based course that looks further at the basic Christian ministry of encouragement; of getting alongside someone and helping them to make progress in Christ	6
So Many Questions	A DVD-based training resource in basic apologetics, including sample answers to 13 common questions	4-10
Where to, Lord?	A DVD-based Bible study on guidance	6
Prayer and the Voice of God	A simple, readable book on this essential topic, with discussion guide	6-10

Option 3

A six-month program to prepare people for a particular ministry (e.g. leading small groups, leading youth group):

Matthias Media Resource	Description	Weeks
The Course of Your Life	A DVD-based course that revolutionizes people's mindset and gives basic training in one-to-one Bible reading	10
Growth Groups	A course for training small group leaders	10
– or –		
No Guts, No Glory	A book and discussion resource for training youth leaders	8-10
– or –		
Their God is So Big	A training course and resource manual for Sunday School teachers	6

For more ideas and more details on the resources mentioned above, visit our website: **www.matthiasmedia.com**

matthiasmedia

Matthias Media is an evangelical publishing ministry that seeks to persuade all Christians of the truth of God's purposes in Jesus Christ as revealed in the Bible, and equip them with high-quality resources, so that by the work of the Holy Spirit they will:

- abandon their lives to the honour and service of Christ in daily holiness and decision-making
- pray constantly in Christ's name for the fruitfulness and growth of his gospel
- speak the Bible's life-changing word whenever and however they can—in the home, in the world and in the fellowship of his people.

It was in 1988 that we first started pursuing this mission, and in God's kindness we now have more than 300 different ministry resources being used all over the world. These resources range from Bible studies and books through to training courses and audio sermons.

To find out more about our large range of very useful resources, and to access samples and free downloads, visit our website:

www.matthiasmedia.com

How to buy our resources

1. Direct from us over the internet:
   - in the US: www.matthiasmedia.com
   - in Australia and the rest of the world: www.matthiasmedia.com.au

*Register at our website for our **free** regular email update to receive information about the latest new resources, **exclusive special offers**, and free articles to help you grow in your Christian life and ministry.*

2. Direct from us by phone:
   - in the US: 1 866 407 4530
   - in Australia: 1800 814 360 (Sydney: 9663 1478)
   - international: +61-2-9663-1478

3. Through a range of outlets in various parts of the world. Visit www.matthiasmedia.com/contact for details about recommended retailers in your part of the world, including www.thegoodbook.co.uk in the United Kingdom.

4. Trade enquiries can be addressed to:
   - in the US and Canada: sales@matthiasmedia.com
   - in Australia and the rest of the world: sales@matthiasmedia.com.au

Looking for something more?

If you're looking for more input for your Christian life and service, take a look at *The Briefing*.

more diversity

With a variety of columns and sections, and local and overseas perspectives, *The Briefing* offers plenty to readers in various stages and walks of life.

more content

Since *The Briefing* is available not just in print but also online, we can provide lots of content, including audio/video and new hosted blogs by gifted Christian thinkers and writers. Choose the content that is most relevant and useful to you.

more convenient

You can receive *The Briefing* in the way that best suits your reading habits—on the web, as an RSS feed, by pdf, as an email update, on your phone or smart device, and of course in print.

more social

Being online, *The Briefing* is share-able and discuss-able. So it's simple to connect your friends into *The Briefing* content via your favourite social networks.

more free

The remarkable thing about *The Briefing* is that it is all available free. Of course, if you want to have the beautiful paper edition mailed out to you then there is a small charge.

more information?

All the information you're likely to need, including subscription options, can be found at:

www.matthiasmedia.com/briefing